Dithyrambs

Books by Richard Katrovas

Prague, USA (Stories, 1996)
The Book of Complaints (1993)
The Public Mirror (1990)
Snug Harbor (1986)
Green Dragons (1983)

Dithyrambs

Choral Lyrics

Richard Katrovas

Carnegie Mellon University Press
Pittsburgh 1998

Acknowledgments

Grateful acknowledgment is made to the following publications in which some of the poems from this volume first appeared:

Denver Quarterly
New Orleans Review
Sycamore Review
Louisiana Literature
Crazy Horse

Special thanks to Bill Lavender, Diane Vance, and Susan Gebhardt.

Cover Art: Marcia Wilderman, adapted from "The Fall of Troy," panel amphora by Lydos, 6th century b.c.

Book and Cover Design: Bill Lavender

Publication of this book is supported by a grant from the Pennsylvania Council on the Arts.

Library of Congress Catalog Card Number 97-65565
ISBN 0-88748-252-X
ISBN 0-88748-253-8 Pbk

10 9 8 7 6 5 4 3 2 1

Contents:

INTRODUCTION

I have little Latin and no Greek, but like a lot of folks I have read the classics in paraphrase and translation, and have always been fascinated by the idea of choral poetry. Of course choral poetry has been attempted in various forms throughout the ages, and arguably a polyvocal aspect is endemic to much High Modernist and postmodernist lyric, but there's not much which seems to attempt (Frost's "masques" come to mind) a reconfiguring, indeed an echoing of ancient choral poetry. That is, the chorus as the tribe's, the polis's deepest reservoir of practical as well as metaphysical wisdom is rarely posited. No less an expert on things ancient and Greek than Gilbert Murray at the turn of the century groused that the choruses in Attic tragedy were little more than a stale convention from an earlier poetic form, and in the context of the actual plays of Aeschylus and Sophocles were to his mind mere nuisances. The wisdom those choruses chanted, danced and sang was, to Murray and others vastly better qualified than I to judge, at best conventional wisdom.

Perhaps for all the wrong reasons, I am enchanted by the choral ejaculations of Attic tragedy, and am fascinated by the question of how tragic drama, the likes of which developed nowhere else on earth, issued from a particular moment in ancient history, the product of satyr plays, dithyrambs, and epics. As far as I can tell, what fragments of dithyrambs we have are not necessarily representative of those immediate precursors of Aeschylus's *Orestia,* and I imagine that one must look directly into Aeschylian drama to see the vestiges of dithyrambs in their latest development, a period when they were original compositions and not simply received, folkish forms.

My dithyrambs are highly stylized blank-verse dramatic mono-logues framed by choral outbursts. In most of them, the male and female choruses are minimal though, I hope, strong presences. In each of these poems, several dialectics are at play, not the least of which is a simultaneous yearning for, and parody of a "high" lyric style.

My choral lyrics, my dithyrambs, are based on dramatic situations similar to what one finds on day-time television; they are at least that melodramatic, that corny. They also speak all I am capable of saying about what it is like to be alive in the twilight of the twentieth century, particularly regarding the relationships between men and women.

Richard Katrovas

QUEEN OF DIAMONDS

FEMALE
CHORUS LEADER: The dreary autumn that I began to bleed,
I dreamed many nights of a gorgeous queen.
Her hair was yellow, her brow translucent,
and her eyes, her eyes were large and aqua-deep.
The nights she loomed beside my bed, her gown
ashimmer with threads as white as diamonds,
it seemed a candle burned beneath her skin.
Each visit, she extended fisted hands.
Sometimes I chose the left one, which always grasped
a dirty piece of string, or razor blade,
but nights I chose the right hand I awoke
before the revelation of its gift.

MALE CHORUS: Praise the street lamps sparkling in shattered glass.
Praise weeds that crack cement in vacant lots.
Praise things that scurry in shadowed alleyways.

FEMALE CHORUS: Sometimes at dawn the eastern sky seems bludgeoned,
as though a god had slammed the skull of night
against the farthest, broadest wall of dark.

FEMALE
CHORUS LEADER: In early spring the dream ceased all at once.
I even tried to will it back, grew sick
for sleeplessness and sorrow at the loss.
Was my queen an angel or a phantom?
Would I never know the gift in her right hand?

FEMALE CHORUS: The moon and stars at dawn are washed away
as though a god hosed down his abattoir.

FEMALE
CHORUS LEADER: Then one blue day that spring I met a girl,
new to the neighborhood and very strange.

Older than I, she had enormous secrets
at which she hinted but would not confess.
I followed after her and always listened.
The boys buzzed around us, ignoring me,
and I observed how regally she brushed
them all aside, and saw she took no joy
in their frenetic fawning, even as
a perverse squint-eyed smile would mar her face
when one would slink slope-shoulderedly away.
Her beauty was a cave I crouched within
throughout the punishing heat of afternoons.

MALE CHORUS
AND FEMALE CHORUS: Praise tender awakenings on summer nights.

FEMALE
CHORUS LEADER: But then she led me to the river bank
and spread a blanket out beneath the stars
so we could watch men paint the sky with fire.
We lay some distance from the lounging crowd,
whose faces flattened, lifted to the dark
as if to catch some dripping dregs of light.
As first blue blossoms wilted in the sky,
the lagging muffled boom rattled through me,
and she turned her head upon my arm, then moved
her fingertips across my flushing throat,
then down and through the buttons of my blouse.

MALE CHORUS: The dazzling lethargy of dying stars,
match-heads dragged slowly on a wall of pitch.

FEMALE CHORUS: Its axis an orthodoxy of the loins,
the language of pleasure eclipses pleasure,
and we are blinded by the aurora ring.

MALE CHORUS
AND FEMALE CHORUS: What lover does not stare upon the sky
and shrink it to dimensions of [his] [her] joy?

9

MALE
CHORUS LEADER:
I passed so many little messages,
a look, a smile, a tender salutation.
Such things do not come easily to me.
But she fills my waking and spills through my sleep.
Her quiet sadness seems too delicate,
too much the essence of abstracted souls
haunting foggy, crowded margins of the world.
We're only colleagues in a little office
training a collective, weary eye on all
the petty transgressions of our company.
It is a vagary of self-policing
that the shiest, least aggressive do the job.
We are sheep who monitor the lives of wolves.
Our office, immaculate if impotent,
hums along from day to day, garnering praise
from those whose bloated budgets we ignore.
Three years her presence in my working life
defines the character of my private hours.
We seem so much alike, yet I cannot say
that repelling force which I so often feel.
What charms me utterly yet holds me off?
What is the fabric of her mystery?

FEMALE
CHORUS LEADER:
Of course her sweetness faded with the season.
She moved on, and on, woman to woman,
a legendary lover of all women
in that hushed community of women
into whose numbers she had ushered me.
I took my own fling at promiscuity,
even a boy or two, but that was show.
I turned prettier with age, sensual,
yet even as I grew more worldly-wise
the torment of my adolescent dream
intensified; what did she represent?
What primal mother love or mother loathing,
or intricate subconscious braiding of
the two did my dream queen most signify?
And what gross trinket of salvation or doom
did that anima of adolescence hide?

MALE CHORUS LEADER:

I know other women, have pleasure with some,
and do not at all live a lonely life.
Family, friends, and occasional lovers
fill my private time, or that much of it
I allow for congenial interaction.
But mostly I prefer to be alone,
though since she soaked into my thoughts and dreams
to be alone in one exquisite pain.
I spend half my working time contriving ways
to brush her arm or smell her subtle scent.
She smiles and chats politely, but that is all.
When once I mustered courage to ask her out,
having rehearsed the casual line for weeks,
she begged off with such cool and stilted grace
I backed away shattered and enchanted.
The Xerox copier shuttles and flashes
between her cubicle and mine; the cooler
gurgles intermittently, and all around
us office romances are blossoming.

FEMALE CHORUS:

From roofs of any city's highest towers,
one may gaze, at dusk, upon the moving glow
of traffic, and office windows going dark
or burning yellow long into the night.

MALE CHORUS:

To love as though one's object of affection
were wholly made of stuff not of this world
is such despicable innocence as gods
inflict upon us for their gross amusement,
being themselves the quintessence of our dreams.

FEMALE CHORUS:

The violence of the maniac who hurts
for mortal fear of tenderness marks off
parameters of heaven's killing floor.
Let gentle-natured men put on their wings
of paraffin and glide into the sun.

Let the anger of men boil in the fat
of their best and worthiest intentions.
Let silly titillation pass no more
for what we need of grave and healing passion.

I know he's smitten, hopelessly in love,
though the hopelessness is rough measurement
less of his capacity for loving
than my self-knowledge and intransigence.
I play with him a little, lead him on
in ways so subtle he doesn't even know.
For all the amusement he affords me,
I've actually mustered some affection for him,
affection born of pity for a fool.
Is there nothing more pathetic than a man
chained to an obsessive, unrequited love?
All the power they stake out in courtship
fizzles faced with feminine disinterest.
Yet there is nothing so tender as women
soon after men have hurt them long and deeply.
I have loved two sweethearts thus afflicted,
taken them in and soothed away the hurt.
Both left for other men, further disaster,
but changed a little for what I gave them,
a heightened capacity for disinterest,
I hope, and memories of slow tenderness.
My office puppy, like most any man,
would change into a monster of disinterest.
I've seen such transformations many times.
Hormonal drives, transferred through the lie
that programs every masculine self-presence,
power a cottage industry of love
which fails soon, leaving women unemployed
or indentured to some bottom line of need.
It's all a matter of passion's timing,
how men begin enthralled but then progress
by swift degrees into desolation,
as women, desolate at birth, journey towards
a dream of utter, unabashed enthrallment.

MALE CHORUS:	Praise the serious words of serious men.
	Praise the wholesome tyrant ranting to a crowd.
	Praise belligerent saints chanting recipes
	for grace to children who are the heart of grace.
	Praise politicians when they tally power
	tapping dollars on their calculators.
	Praise the piercing minds of acerbic wits
	compensating for secret, withered lives.
	Praise demented heroes of forgotten wars
	braying epithets at their radios.
	Praise the cop who beats the kid who shot the kid
	who sold the drugs that killed the kid who shot
	the cop who kicked and beat the kid who sold
	the drugs that killed the kid who shot the kid
	who knifed the kid who broke his mother's heart.
FEMALE CHORUS:	Praise shivering breadths of scattered city lights.
	Praise muted voices in a crowded room.
	Praise sacred rage of children much abused.
	Praise ministers of doom on television.
	Praise conspiracies of righteousness.
	Praise the distance that a leaf must carry
	blown fluttering across a bright autumnal sky.
	Praise hands of a woman lifted against the hand
	that hangs clenched upon the air above her.
MALE	
CHORUS LEADER:	The essence of it I know is quite unreal,
	unreal as well the urge which is no more
	than relentless forces channeled by the vague
	arbitrary rules of sweet engagement.
	Even at its gentlest, pursuit of love
	so often feels a predatory act.
	No doubt my boyish, shy fixation hides
	the fierce self-loathing of a man too meek
	to alter circumstances of his life.
	It is, perhaps, just cowardly diversion.

Yet who does not feel recreated in the flesh
when love's delusions flair upon the brain?
The cultivated lie which first released
the civilizing power of hope for change
tethers still the human will to phantoms.
We who are doomed know we are doomed, yet dance
out on the shimmering brink of destiny,
as though the progress into nothingness
proceeds according to the mandates of
not actuary tables, but fairy tales.

FEMALE
CHORUS LEADER: That day, I hope when I am very old,
I rasp my final breaths upon the world,
my queen of diamonds, more ravishing
and splendid than my adolescent dreams
could ever have contrived, will turn her wrist
so blue, delicate veins are visible,
and her fingers will uncurl like tendrils.
I know this as I know a gentle rain
may signify implicit boundaries of
a flower dying towards its loveliest
moment, as though disaster is its own
reward for all living things, sentient or not.

MALE CHORUS
AND FEMALE CHORUS: The slow, insistent pull of gentle starlight,
like old friends who guide you from a stool
that you may reel through doors onto the night,
precedes collapse of will and vertigo
of terror, as the final hour expires.

FEMALE CHORUS: By mysterious inversion, in men's dreams
women's naked bodies are emblems of death.

MALE
CHORUS LEADER: I am one thing in pursuit, quite another
when I've achieved what I pursued, yet all
the sweetness promised by the fantasy
prepares a lover's palate for a taste
of something only precincts of heaven
may concoct, and to know this is a torment.

14

Yet as a form of play distracting from
the needs and thoughts which sanctify denial,
the game of Sex and Death is always lost
by virtue of a quick repatriation
of flames to Republics of the Sun,
as passion recalled, in desolate fields
of passion spent, is daylight flashing on
great banked and sparkling rifts of virgin snow.

THE CHILD

MALE AND
FEMALE CHORUS:

We shimmer through gilt surfaces of mist,
or flit and buzz upon the stink of waste.
As clouds to granite peaks, or sex to death,
we are the essence of what faith conceals.

MALE
CHORUS LEADER:

Lucid to the end, my bright little one
listened to the old stories, her hair fanned out
over the pillow, her dark eyes intent
upon the ceiling; I tried to say the words
with all the cheer her innocence required,
to make the fables serve as verbal bond
between a father's need and daughter's wonder.
But as I mouthed the words and watched her face
drain away that quick, sustained enchantment
defining by its purity all hope,
even before the light had left her eyes
I knew she was no more the child I'd loved.

FEMALE CHORUS:

Praise the lies which are our consolations.

MALE
CHORUS LEADER:

A quiet wisdom filled her tortured gaze,
as though inside that moment before death
profundity was revealed that washed away
all innocence, and left her dull and sated.
I read on, several pages, to the end,
the happy ending of a fairy tale
in which the princess blah blah blah blah blah,
after I knew my little girl was gone.

MALE CHORUS:

Praise the cold lights of cities far away.
Praise stars that are the daughters of all darkness.

There is nothing left between us, yet still
we scavenge the ruins of the other.
I take his hand in the night, and squeeze, as though
small intimacies still were possible.
No joy, not even old sardonic humor
of memories saved against such pain as this
suffices, for as our present bleeds into
a future of intolerable loss,
so our past is now intolerable.
We mumble over meals of starting over,
of other children who may compensate.
But we know there is no compensation.
We are lost within the details of our loss,
and live not together, but juxtaposed.

FEMALE CHORUS: Praise all our burdens larger than the sky.
Praise delicate shavings of our wooden hearts.
Praise deaf, mute angels who graze among the beasts.

FEMALE
CHORUS LEADER: I was contented with their special closeness,
which didn't exclude so much as ignore.
I knew she might flit between us for years,
favoring one and then the other, until
she danced away, and we became one thing,
her single point from which to keep a distance.
As she grew ill, she called for him in the day,
but after dark for me. I was her sleep,
her sole diversion from the swelling terror.

MALE
CHORUS LEADER: The world we made was sweeter than the world,
more just, of course, but also filled with dangers,
quite insurmountable it seemed, except
for our deus ex machina, her magic.
When trolls or giants threatened her, a wave
of wand or other charming trinket pressed
into the service of her will saved worlds.

Such power as hers a father might envy, but
that his child, his truest love, possessed it.

FEMALE CHORUS:

If suddenly you wake, alone and scared
to be alone, consider coldly the hour
of your passing, the hurt breathing, prolonged
by the body's will, other than your own,
or that it happens violently, the glass
splashing all around, the buckling steel,
and concussion like a drum: you are the drum.

MALE CHORUS:

Praise neon flash against the pitch of night.
Praise laughter stumbling through an unlit morning.
Praise boys in bodies of strong men cursing
the first fay light, then falling to their knees.

FEMALE
CHORUS LEADER:

I stare at him across a room. He reads.
He wets his finger, flips the page. The sun-
light edging through the curtain streaks and blanches
one ruddy cheek and baggy eye. He blinks
and squints a bit against the light, the light
which in a moment softens, slips away.
He shifts his glasses, glances at the clock,
rises painfully, pads into the den.
The clink, the click, the popping of the cubes,
the long fall into fitful sleep in which
he often thrashes, weeps, and moans her name.

MALE AND
FEMALE CHORUS:

Consider stepping slowly into flames
as though to do so were a luxury.

FEMALE CHORUS:

Praise the waxed corridors of public buildings.
Praise the frowns and furrowed brows of specialists.
Praise hothouse flowers in almost every window.

MALE CHORUS:	Praise those who suffer unabashedly.
FEMALE CHORUS:	Praise those who curl up in the dark and weep.
MALE CHORUS:	Praise those who weep as though to weep forever.
FEMALE CHORUS:	Praise suicide in verdant, quiet places.
MALE CHORUS:	Praise all who suffer life to live, and live.

MALE
CHORUS LEADER:

I have held the tart barrel on my tongue,
a sentimental gesture, yes, and quite
irrelevant, or, at least, self-mocking.
The pain of loss is all I have of her.
To lose myself would be to lose even that.
And this is not a coward's consolation.
When the pain is exhausted, frazzled, numb,
I'll take the quick ride on eternity.

FEMALE
CHORUS LEADER:

I've grown concerned beyond my own shrill pain.
I trace the contours of his thoughts against
his will, and know they burn, shriek, and dovetail
with a single image, then arc upon
a flash of longing into oblivion.

FEMALE AND
MALE CHORUS:

Inscribed upon the brutish heart of each
self-marvelling, foolish man are litanies
of crimes he would contrive if world were blind.
The wish to fill a universe completely,
supplant all matter, subsume all light, until

there is only the one masculine will
throbbing upon, within, about itself,
determines heft and depth of lyric sorrow.
For where but in the fixed command to breed
resides the hell and bliss of what we are?
Those who rescue beauty, love, and pride
from the reeking pit of procreation
will simulate the dateless birth of God,
and know too late the pit itself divine.

FEMALE CHORUS: What lies are these we tally in our dreams?

MALE CHORUS: What dreams are these in which we stow our sins?

FEMALE CHORUS: May victims plead no more with evil men.
May false dawns kiss no more the fields of death.
May cries recede to the hushed banks of sleep.

MALE CHORUS: Praise the great river from which all sorrow flows.

FEMALE CHORUS: Praise redundant rains that swell the river.

MALE CHORUS: Praise reciprocity of rains and rivers.

FEMALE
CHORUS LEADER: Our marriage was not born of romance, but then
our lives were bound by stronger promises
than tether those ephemeral affections
wilder hearts will rue when passions cool.
We grew into a comfort that soon slipped
into a numbness not at all unpleasant.
He seemed to need so little of me, and I
required his acquiescent presence only.
A decade passed. A piece of another turned

it seemed to mist and blew away. The grave,
I guess, seemed not imminent, but closer, close
enough, quite suddenly it seemed, for him,
I say it seemed for him, but not for me,
that we should open out our lives and try
to make a life to haunt when we are gone.

FEMALE CHORUS: Praise news of death we read in children's eyes.

MALE
CHORUS LEADER: I did not resent her need for comfort,
and respected always the sacrifice
she made to drop the child into our lives.
It was a gift, I knew, from her to me,
beyond implicit contracts we had forged,
a friendship token I was grateful for,
and promised solemnly to bear the weight
of nasty little daily infamies.
But through the pregnancy she changed.
The act begun abstractly as accretion,
a waiting for a process too complex
to understand except in orcadest terms,
became a mystery she took to heart.

MALE CHORUS: Praise all the changes of the protean heart.

MALE
CHORUS LEADER: And so the child was hers through birth and after,
and I was household helper, hired hand
to fetch and tote and clear up after them.
And I was happy, happy in the role,
and marvelled at the bond, the natural bond
between a woman's and an infant's needs.
To my consciousness, they became an it,
a single thing outside of us yet still
within such intimate proximity
we danced in fixed and elegant orbit of
the same cosmic consequences, the same
vague, magnificent, fate-filled potency.

FEMALE CHORUS: May love become a grave contingency.

MALE CHORUS: Praise miles of dirt packed thick with bulbs and seeds.

FEMALE CHORUS: May myths of love not blur the thing itself.

MALE CHORUS: Praise the harvest! Praise abundance! Praise life!

FEMALE
CHORUS LEADER: It was in language he made his bond with her.
                   In myths and legends, explanations of
                   the pictures in the books he read aloud
                   each night, his voice became the voice of time,
                   and voice of naming things, and how they work,
                   and why, and why and why and why and why.
                   When she was barely old enough to talk,
                   when she could barely talk they talked for hours.
                   His interest never flagged; he sat and calmly
                   listened, then calmly answered every question,
                   or simply nodded affirmation as
                   she babbled on from point to childish point.
                   He repossessed his world, through words, through her.
                   And as she grew into the language, past
                   babble into a reasoned, smart regard
                   of fabula and what she daily witnessed,
                   so his world deepened such that what had been
                   vexations, horrors, threats, affronts and schemes
                   became in sum the mystery of life,
                   that which he would prepare her for before
                   he passed from mystery to mystery.

FEMALE AND
MALE CHORUS: Praise heart's surrender to the small and mild.

22

His silence now is haunted by her voice.
He listens to each word she doesn't say.
My heart may not surrender to her loss
as long as I must mourn his mourning her.
I walk out to the garden, touch each rose,
pick away a few dead leaves, caress a thorn.
Magnolias nod their gaudy blooms like old
bewitching mothers soon to curl, and die.
They are so much clumsier than the roses.
Yet I love them more than any flower.
I love the rich creaminess of their petals.
I love how comical they are in death,
their rotting skins hugging to the compost
like happy drunkards singing to themselves.
My baby's gone, and legions of roses spill
their sexual softness after her upon
the huge and perfect lap that death becomes.

THE DANCER

FEMALE CHORUS:
Because the core of all we are is time,
we turn, demure, and turn again to face
the monster, prince, magician, or good swain
and turn again, precisely, flit and shudder
to signify a woman's hopelessness.

MALE CHORUS:
Before music, word, or figure was the dance.
To turn, and turning change from thing to thing
obsessed with where it is and where it goes,
to turn, and turning burn with righteousness
requires we sharpen vision on the heart
that memory may pierce the oldest longings
and know the first contortions of things in time.

MALE
CHORUS LEADER:
When finally she lets me watch her dance,
she's been my concubine for seven years,
that is, I've been her steady customer
for long enough she finds me comforting;
so "concubine," of course, is irony,
because "steady" need not imply exclusive.
But in my heart she is my concubine,
my sweet purveyor of the darkest pleasures.
I say "my heart" and wince, for if it is
my heart she so affects it throbs between
my thighs, not tucked within my sunken chest.

FEMALE CHORUS:
So it is with puerile satisfaction;
the men's affections get displaced while those
of women are transfigured or ignored.

FEMALE
CHORUS LEADER:
For seven years he's begged to watch me dance.
Why now I bring him here I cannot say.
When he first phoned my partner, said he'd pay
a thousand bucks to do a ballerina,

24

my boy Sweet Donny laughed until she wheezed,
then said no problem, such a girl would show
at Breaker's Inn, Room fifty-two, at nine.
Then Donny made me put my toeshoes on,
and under my coat I wore white leotard.
Inside, he took one look and gravely asked
if fifth position pointed in or out.
I posed in fifth, then moved to third, then first
mechanically, bored, a little mad
that such a silly test could verify
what anyone who loves the art can know
by checking out my perfect form, how years
of classes, two a day two hours each,
sculpt a body predisposed to shaping.
And if the ballet master's good, if she
or he was trained in Russian style and keeps
good faith with rigors of that austere method,
a woman's body over years becomes
pure diamond, her delicate facets ablaze.
As for performance, well, I am too old
for that dream. It is the studio I love.
Girls, some gay boys, fewer straight, will work
for love, the comradeship, the joy and pain
of high physical standards that can't be faked.
That first night all we did was talk of it.
He'd seen Fonteyn do Juliet past forty,
and swore he never doubted her a girl.
And Balanchine he didn't doubt loved women,
though such love was sick, and sick the art it made.

MALE CHORUS: Praise women's bodies singing silently.

FEMALE CHORUS: May bodies lose particularity.

MALE CHORUS: Praise lurid swans who die into their beauty.

MALE
CHORUS LEADER: Her peroxide hair drawn back so black roots trace
her scalp, mascara so thick against her pale,

powdery pale skin her eyes seem painted on.
She stretches at bar, glancing in the mirror
like the rest, and like them losing sense of self
to gods of pure technique and symmetry.
Ballet aesthetic needs annihilation
of the "soul," for if musician gives all
to instrument, her selfhood still remains
as agent, for even singer makes a thing
of human voice, and remains an agent of
that otherness, but where indeed is that which
moves the body when the body, whole, is slave,
is instrument, is perfect puppet for
so many others' fantasies and wishes?
Choreographers, studio instructors,
fleshy mamas dreaming through their skinny girls,
appropriate what of the dance is art,
that is, volition, subtlety and tact.
When all is execution of a will
outside the executing self, where is
the danger art implies beyond mere ritual?

FEMALE CHORUS: May flower turning to a light be measure
of grace, and grace be measure of all worth.

MALE CHORUS: Praise life, the beautiful mistake of nature,
and praise all beauty in the name of death.

FEMALE AND
MALE CHORUS: As forces other than the self dictate
what body is, becomes, has done, will do,
is not the grace with which it acquiesces—
how well it is determined— what we are
when skillful, wise, detached, and beautiful?
No beauty comes from struggles with our fates.
The beauty of the tragic is protracted
recognition of the hero's folly,
what he comes to know of it and how with grace
he lives in truth, and loves humiliation.

26

He made a date for every second Tuesday
of each month, and so for seven years
he's partnered me, and paid a handy sum,
less partner, then, than patron of the arts.
He says my body hasn't lost a thing,
the muscle tone remains exquisite, firm
and lean, as though taut ropes beneath my skin,
my sallow skin, run my willowy length.
He is obsessed with every speck of me,
each contour, groove, smooth or hairy hollow,
and inspects me as no man ever has.
I don't explain my nicks and bruises to him.
He knows what occupational hazards are,
and simply worships each month at my form.
And so our time reveals he does not love
the art so much as he is kept amazed
by the world of us who live inside ballet,
not prodigious babies of great companies,
the young who make a living for a while
being almost perfect on the stage
for gaudy asses sitting on new money,
rather the real world of ballet, the one
where bodies sweat, dreaming of perfection,
performing for the mirrors and each other,
and where the body longs in pain for beauty,
in daily ceremonies of submission.
He loves my body, as a thing to love
and as an abstract notion he cannot name,
an idea he's struggled with his life to know.
Of course with men it comes to thoughts of death,
in the end, always, it comes to fear of death.

MALE CHORUS: Praise small winds that sway the trees in darkness.

FEMALE CHORUS: As every blossom turns its head to light
and withers back to nothingness alone,
no blossom mourns for blossoms when they fade.

27

**MALE
CHORUS LEADER:**   At center now, they pace through first routine
as a little Slavic tyrant claps the time
and barks the moves and scans them with a scowl.
Clearly, hers ranks among the better bodies,
though her technique is merely mediocre.
She said that two young girls she works out with
have toured with East Coast companies, and I
can see already who they are. They both
seem nineteen, maybe twenty; I'd wager
they grew up in velvet suburbs, daddies'
little girls, amiable, a little dumb,
but early on so obviously gifted
with handsome bodies and a knack for moving.
Perhaps they have not read a book between them,
watch hours of television and their weights
and could not spell Tchaikovsky for their lives.
Can such as they be artists? Though their technique
is quite precise, where's the life behind it?
Or am I foolish to assume a life
may shudder forth from shadows of techne?
My love, my concubine, so loves the art
it shows especially in her imperfections.
In her straining after what those girls achieve
with ease, she represents the common lot
of unheroic, gross humanity.

MALE CHORUS: Praise aging satyrs posing in the fields.
Praise impotence which is the core of mercy.
Praise men who live beyond their youths to know
the rank necessity of frequent weeping.

FEMALE CHORUS: May all who live for beauty stand within
the chance parameters of shifting dreams
of meaning, healing where the world is quiet.
May such as they learn to move with feeling,
and may every seeker of the beautiful
require a perfect mirror for confessions
wept in unambiguous, total darkness.

CHORUS LEADER: Seven years of humping the little guy
and still I don't know very much about him.
I know he's rich, or "comfortable," as
he puts it, achieved this blessed state a bit
by his own skill, but mostly from a dead
and childless aunt who'd bought a town in Texas.
His progeny matriculate at pricey
ivy-clotted colleges, study death.
His wife's a mouse with money of her own;
she cultivates her ignorance, and lives
a separate, pleasant, if unhappy life.
He watches from the balcony, perhaps
enthralled, though more likely disappointed.
I'm not deluded; I know I'm not that good.
I simply love the discipline of dance.
I bear my mediocrity with honor.
Technique exists apart from human genius;
aspiring to perfection is enough,
indeed in this is like all worshiping.
I worship, then, perfection with my body.
And he, poor fool, through me, also worships it,
as though my hard, slim body were an altar
to perfection wholly disembodied,
ideal yet real, corporeal yet ether.

FEMALE CHORUS: May all who live in truth be recognized
as angels of their time, and garner much
affection; for all who live in truth are blessed.

MALE
CHORUS LEADER: In centuries passed, the female dancers lived
often poor, disgraceful lives, even as
on stage they represented every virtue
of femininity and female beauty.
After most performances, gentlemen
would gather in the Green Room, as though it were
a place of auction, and bid their favorite ones.
And many dancers, because they worked all day
at jobs that paid them poorly just to dance

at night, would proffer favors to the men.
The lucky ones became the mistresses
of wealthy, solid lovers of the arts,
and so continued dancing undistracted.
The man who loves a dancer loves a space
between the present and the absent self,
the blank daughter of entropy and stasis.

MALE CHORUS: Praise underground economies of flesh,
for they are ancient, simple and enduring.

FEMALE CHORUS: May slaves make slaves of masters whom they love.

FEMALE
CHORUS LEADER: I am his wish for immortality,
his cowards' secret self-consuming passion.
But I am first my own concealed despair,
and when I dance the dance is dream of bliss
I dance within, neither affirming nor
denying the dream itself, though that bliss,
which is the subject of the dream, I mock
with every predetermined gesture of
my body, and that precisely is my "soul."
I am just a dancer, and love no man.

THE MURDERER

FEMALE CHORUS:

Each night the hands of God are on our throats,
for from the Word of God the Wrath of God
must issue out upon the sleep of women.

MALE CHORUS:

God's proxies at the borders of their sleep,
we fill the empty spaces there with words.

FEMALE
CHORUS LEADER:

I did not know what loathing was until
my vision fell upon his living face
at last, so different from the photographs.
To see him enter placidly, shackled
and cuffed, his orange prison uniform pressed
and almost glowing in its obscene happy
flash of Halloween associations,
to see him blink, then smile familiarly
at the tight-lipped lawyer handling his defense,
is then to see within myself his hands
upon my daughter's body, those hands I see
now rendered wrist to wrist, almost delicate,
and wish with all this mother's body I
might with my own hands choke his wretched life.

MALE CHORUS:

Praise the heart that burns for retribution.
Praise the heart whose conflagration is revenge.

MALE
CHORUS LEADER:

This system by which monsters know their rights
mandates I represent him as I would
a righteous soul petitioning for bliss.
I advocate for him as if his life
were mine, and so therefore it is, and I
shall by the law protect him as if he
were something precious, so worthy of my life.
I look at him and see a pleasant face
like any other sunny one I meet

on daily passages through streets and rooms.
Though over thirty, he has a boyish charm,
an easy smile and easy sense of humor.
If I can prove confessions were coerced—
for murders in this state—I grant him time,
and time is all he wants or needs from me.
He'll move on then to another state for trial,
another legal ruse to buy him time:
his currency, commodity, and wealth.
It has become a game for him, a small
diversion from the bleakness of his cell.
He knows he'll die in prison; the game is when,
for how he'll die is technicality.
He joked last week of when he was a boy
and stuck a pin into an empty socket.
The feeling wasn't all that bad, he said.

FEMALE CHORUS:

May unrepentant monster fix his gaze
upon his open hands unto his death.
May every man look on the monster's eyes
and see himself and every man who's lived.
May every man embrace the monster once,
and learn to weep for it and for himself.

FEMALE
CHORUS LEADER:

Her dream was that one day she'd own a shop,
a "chic boutique" somewhere the rich would feel
comfortable browsing and taking their time
to make the perfect purchase of the day.
She loved the rich, or how she thought they lived.
But she was dull, too sweet, too modest even
to think that she might someday count herself
among them, so she dreamed proximity.
The day she worked up nerve to tell her dad
and me she'd found a studio uptown
where she could keep her cat and see the park
from the eastern window, my heart sank with pride.
We didn't want her then to go, but she
was twenty, had a job and needed space
and solitude to love and grow beyond us.
Not even a month had passed. We'd talked each night
on the phone more than we ever had at home,
and joked how moving apart had made us close.

I spoke at least nine times to her machine
before I felt nauseous alarm and drove
past midnight to her place and used the key
I knew she kept beneath a potted plant.

FEMALE CHORUS: May what we cannot help but love too much
                   not die into mere myth of heart's excess.

FEMALE
CHORUS LEADER: Her life with us transported to that room
                   was eerily assuring; knickknacks arranged
                   in similar fashion to how they'd graced
                   her room, the very furniture the same,
                   even her stuffed animals, whose names of course
                   I knew, grazed upon her grandmother's quilt
                   in the same configuration as when
                   she'd talked to them in earnest dialogue.
                   From calm reconnaissance of familiar things
                   a jolt of recognition shook me hard.
                   I saw the things that signified her life
                   of sheltered comfort, I saw her innocence,
                   and knew I'd raised a victim for the world,
                   a woman without guile or understanding
                   of fundamental evils everywhere.
                   My mother's heart clenched against the knowledge
                   that we had failed to shape her understanding
                   of just how thin is veneer of civilized
                   behavior, and that for each victim lost
                   wandering the dark, a predator awaits.

MALE CHORUS: Praise the stalker smoldering in his skin.
                   Praise indifference of the sparkling sky.
                   Praise the witnessing stars and vegetation.

FEMALE CHORUS: May she in throes of terror see beyond
                   her torment to the coming calm, and sleep.

FEMALE AND
MALE CHORUS: What is this sickness of the self that numbs

it to what loins compel the hands to hurt?
What is this sickness of the loins that kills
the soul, or that small part which rules compassion?
May it be some vestige of the racial past,
an atavistic memory lolling in
the blood, perhaps mutated into something
that but manifests as odd confusion
of a hunter's social role and mating drives?
Because each body's actions are a true
identity, a conscious being may
not play the monster and not be a monster.

MALE
CHORUS LEADER: The many hours now that I have spent
with him, in stark booths of steel and plastic
that serve as legal border to our lives,
have reinforced that strained allegiance formed
between a brutal killer and his council.
"How many?" once I asked off-handedly.
He smiled, as if to show surprise that I
should be so unprofessional as to pose
a question for my own, not the case's, sake.
"Nineteen, I guess," he answered, and did not blink.
All women, all young and pretty, all killed
by strangulation as he raped them, all
daughters grieved, some wives or lovers grieved.
I brought him cigarettes and magazines,
outlined the case, and was impressed by how
attentive was his eye for legal details,
and how acute his mind for strategies.
His questions cogent and his voice sincere,
he was my partner in a project less
a matter of his life than a game that gave
a temporary, facile meaning to it.
There was indeed civility to how
we worked together, a mutual respect
I found grotesque yet unavoidable.
One time, wholly unsolicited, he asked
if ever I have wondered what it's like.
The referent in his question glittered in
his eyes, and I grew sick, my stomach burned,
but what revolted me was not that he

34

could ask the question, but that I could not
respond without his seeing in my eyes
the undeniable true answer, yes.

FEMALE CHORUS: May guilt remain a matter of what men
and women do, and not what they may dream.
May every man permit himself to dream
atrocities, and punish them himself
with further dreams of wretched retribution.
Let no man think that he holds not within
himself all human monsters who have racked
the innocent and meager of the earth.
Specific guilt is general, and gross.

MALE CHORUS: Contingencies bleed contingencies, blind codes
replicate, and the human heart grows bloated,
abstract, irrelevant, distracted, and sweet.
The human monster eats the human heart.

FEMALE
CHORUS LEADER: Where they found her, how they found her, when
and why they found her, and what we said or screamed
or wept ran on the local news that day,
and then again that night with commentary.
Her glowing proud face from a prom night photo
flashed over and over, and "tragedy"
was mouthed again and again, but her poor death,
so pathetic, humiliating, lacked
the simple dignity of tragic life.
The lamb to slaughter is no tragic victim.

MALE CHORUS: Praise all who pass stark lucid from this life.

FEMALE CHORUS: May fading light diminish violent pain.

MALE
CHORUS LEADER: I thought I'd put his mother on the stand
in hope that stories of a troubled child

abused by father, teachers, anyone
would dampen coals of general opinion.
But when I quizzed him on his family
he laughed, and said they were good Christians all.
They prayed, quite surely, each night for his soul.
No juicy family nightmares there, he laughed,
no explanations for his evil acts.
When he said "evil," the word had resonance.
I could not help but ask him what he meant.
In other words, was evil real to him,
or was it synonym for antisocial,
sick, misguided, or just misunderstood?
He paused and looked away, then cleared his throat.
He said that evil is more real than good,
if real is what we call what we may see
and touch and reconcile to daily life.
The good, he said, is palpable abstraction,
though soon as it is touched it turns to cloud,
and blows across a landscape of desire.
I knew then that he was my special teacher,
and that self-knowledge cost as least as much
as what discomfort he had caused me when
I was impressed by his humanity.
For evil is attractive when sincere.
But then I only had to imagine hands
upon a woman's throat, or more to the point,
imagine staring up into his eyes
as his hands choked off air and voice from me.
So thus it is imagination serves
to clarify perspective, rinse away
blurring gloss of abstract speculation
from the breath and blood of life's true judgments.
Evil is imagination's failure
to empathize with innocent and weak,
the will to power unmediated by
a deep compulsion to imagine pain
of those the will obliterates that it
may be, and grow, and justify itself.
The good man is but conflicted monster, one
who feels the consequences of his acts
before committing them, so does not act.

FEMALE CHORUS: May each man dream his life another one.
                   May each be humbled by the world's slow will.

FEMALE
CHORUS LEADER: How may a parent not lie awake and see
                   the violence her child suffered unto death,
                   see it through the child's own eyes? Did she scream
                   for me, her father, or for God, and when
                   no one answered as the pain increased
                   and terror crested, did she feel forsaken?

MALE CHORUS: Praise the tide of sleep that washes over pain.

FEMALE
CHORUS LEADER: Surely she closed her eyes and became my child,
                   relaxed small creature I grew inside of me.
                   Surely that dark was warm, familiar, good.

FEMALE CHORUS: May innocence be shield for innocence.

MALE
CHORUS LEADER: The paper printed pictures of the girls,
                   whose bodies had been found, in a long row.
                   I tore it out and keep it in my wallet.
                   I unfold the little wedge and stare at them
                   several times a day, and know the others,
                   the ones he strings the cops along about,
                   would look no different, would smile above the print
                   on prom nights, birthdays, or sweet sixteens,
                   their hair puffed up, their eyes made deep with liner.
                   What scientific explanation can
                   be marshalled to the horrors of their deaths?
                   What blown neural filaments had set
                   him spinning out beyond sane sense of self?
                   What childhood traumas can account for him?
                   And what if he's as sane as anyone?

If I had it in my hands to kill him,
I would only do it facing eye to eye,
for it could only please me if I saw
the pain and shock contort his face
and fill the air with deathward plunging shrieks.
How I wish that I could make him suffer.
Yet irony of deepest mother love
is that to mourn in earnest is to love
profoundly, and such a love abhors revenge.
What then the world or agent of it takes
from what of you is mother, you must love
as loathing may be love of what is gone
when absence is intensity of presence.
I look at him and see a lonely man.

THE PRESIDENT

FEMALE CHORUS: May none ignore biology of power.

MALE CHORUS: Praise public icons as they lay in pieces.

FEMALE CHORUS: There's power in the mask that grants us power.

MALE CHORUS: Interrupted cycles reveal new patterns.

FEMALE CHORUS: Untethered from time we enter history,
as only bleeding bodies live in time,
and history is a power out of time,
as words are power over thought in time.

MALE
CHORUS LEADER: She won election with a stirring mandate.
In this she was like every other hack
who blathers slogans for the nightly news.
What made her different was that she was change.
I sat with colleagues in our favorite bar
and joked about the sex change in the Ovary
Office, and whether she would grace the House
with more or less intrigue than all the men
whose horny shades would surely harass her.
But one among us didn't laugh; she said
she thought our comments typical of men,
and this of course set the bar to roaring.
She walked away with anger in her gait,
and though I laughed along with all the others
I felt a twinge of sympathy for her,
and paused a moment to reflect upon
what a woman president must mean to her,
then told a joke about the farmer's daughter,
the one in which the salesman buys a pig.

FEMALE CHORUS: May those who love frivolity beware
disasters that foment in sadder places.

FEMALE
CHORUS LEADER: In office for a month and I am burdened
with secrets full of doom and dread despair,
but none like this for which I must decide
to end three million lives in one great flash
or chance a war in which the world may die.
Of course I know what I must do; within
an hour of my call the act is done.
I hesitate because I hear the breaths
of children, sleeping now, who will be sleeping
still when it occurs, and wish that I could
gather them up and take them somewhere quiet.
But no more quiet places on the earth
still shelter innocence; the world is loud
with masculine revenge and consternation.
The best that I can do for children there
is to annihilate them while they sleep.

MALE CHORUS: Praise all brave leaders who are resolute.

FEMALE
CHORUS LEADER: The call is made, the deed as good as done.

MALE
CHORUS LEADER: Her words were slow and grave; the room was hushed.
Long seconds passed before a network star
rose to ask a question; it seemed he had
not grasped what she had said, so yet again
she outlined what at midnight in that time zone
had occurred, just minutes ago in ours.
The star went pale, imploded slowly, sat.
I rose and asked how long before assessments
of the damage would be possible; she shook
her head and said she really didn't know.
Surely, a print correspondent yelled from near

the back, satellite reconnaissance reveals
to what extent the devastation spread.
But then she shook her head and stared at him
an odd long length of TV silent time,
and assured him devastation was complete.
She ended simply by repeating how
the situation was impossible,
swift action was imperative, and nothing
prepares a leader for decisions that
proceed from situations of no choice.
What have our words become when instant deaths
of millions constitute a situation?
What kind of monsters wagered all that she
could not do what her predecessors would?
What were the odds of global conflagration?
How will the world react, but more important,
how will markets take the news tomorrow?
Millions in an instant, and she was there
as surely as the man who flipped the switch.
A word, or two or three, and millions gone.

FEMALE AND
MALE CHORUS: With grave responsibility despair
must live, and she who executes grave power
may only hope for history's redemption.

FEMALE
CHORUS LEADER: Athena bursting from her father's brow
intrigued me as I sauntered off to school.
My daddy's girl, I stormed the Ivy League
shieldless, no helmet, but ready for a fight.
I loved three men, two women, one idea.
Power, what it means, how it happens,
where and when it manifests in human
intercourse was for me that star a German
said each good mind must choose and fix upon.
I studied power as my sisters studied love.
I thought for many years that power was freedom,
and that a woman to be free must have
the active, clean, unmediated power
to live conterminous, not entangled,
with louder lives of men, and in such a way

41

that brother left unburied by proud tyrant
should never force a stifling martyrdom.
I was my father's daughter; I loved him well,
and knew that if I were to have a life
worthy of his love I had to kill him,
more like a loathing son than doting daughter,
and to his credit, he bared his heart to me
as to an enemy much loved, and I,
my quiet mother's proxy, cut it out
of him in a dream of tribal passage
unto a stage of power much revered.
I entered politics to win, and won.

FEMALE CHORUS: The long dirt road, dusty and clotted with lives
fleeing, is the metaphor of our time.
Our lives are the road, and dying children on
it are precisely what we cannot tell
our dear little ones in their little beds.
Who touches her sleeper's exquisite face
touches too the hollow cheeks of misery.
Every child brings us to all children.

FEMALE
CHORUS LEADER: Childless, past menopause, I mother nothing.
Yet I am mother to a nation, now.

MALE CHORUS: When she who bore us passes from this life
we must absorb her finer aspects as
all love consumes what had occasioned it.

FEMALE CHORUS: May she who suffers consequences of
grave deeds not suffer too men's cowardice.

MALE CHORUS: Praise power's wisdom that knows no gender,
for wisdom may be judgment unknotted from
procreation's monotonous agenda.
That is the purchase of the old on wisdom.

FEMALE
CHORUS LEADER: I'm told my numbers in the polls are good.
The nation "understands," "condones," "supports"
the act, and even markets surge to show
captains of industry and all their minions
will rally to the skirt of stark resolve.
My stomach churns; if I could fade tonight
into a bliss of guiltless slumber never
to wake, I would shed my name and station
for anonymity among the stars.
But I am not a coward, and now must seek
redemption on the stage of public life.
My critics, few but vocal, call it murder.
And when the first true pictures hit TV
masses who support the deed in principle
will sit slack-jawed, and ruminate upon
the actual horror and destruction there,
and only then will public sentiment
turn introspective, and jingoism fade,
for in America a thing's not real
until it's seen, nor has event occurred
which does not blaze in stark and graphic detail.
The new device was very clean, I'm told;
contamination therefore will be quite
contained, especially given that the weather
there was quite conducive to containment.
He modified each adjective with quite,
that blinking man who briefed us on effects.
I heard myself, as though another, ask
if there was any pain, and all around
the conference table a shocked hush shivered
in the somber faces of trusted friends and foes,
as the loyal little bureaucrat pushed
his sagging glasses with a shaking finger
off his sweaty nose and then explained
that most returned to nothing instantly,
but as for those who lived at farthest points
he could not say, but if he had to guess,
it was likely some had suffered briefly.
I stared at him and did not say a word.
It seemed he verged on shattering into tears.
I ended silence with some solemn words

about the world and how it's changed and still
may change, and how America must lead.
No madmen with designs on greater power
will ever threaten lightly with a few
jerryrigged devices, nor hide behind
brutalized innocence of their people's lives.
I dismissed them all, and sat alone, and wept.

MALE CHORUS: The paradox of power is that it weighs
upon the good heart ten times heavier
than on the evil one, and yet the good
compelled to have it are siblings to evil,
for all evil is power without conscience,
and power's acquisition, even for
the good, requires conscience in abeyance.

MALE
CHORUS LEADER: I saw my colleague in the bar last night.
She drank alone, and with deliberate speed.
I watched her knock back three stiff doubles and chase
them with a draft, as though it were a task
assigned, and she would never disappoint.
She gave permission, so I took the stool
beside her, ordered call brand bourbon, asked
her how her day had passed. She didn't answer
for a moment, then asked if I was kidding.
I asked her how she felt, and was not joking
this time and she knew it, so she said
she felt as though all sweetness had been drained
from life, nor would be plentiful again.
She did not blame the president, yet thought
as well the world had for the first time known
mass destruction from a woman's hand, and so
her gender, in a modern sense, had lost
an innocence whose loss may be redemption,
and yet redemption at a dreadful price.
The small brutalities of dailiness
would haunt and vex the lives of women still,
but now she felt a sick complicity
with all the monsters of the brutal ages
whereas before she'd felt a moral distance.
She said she'd tried to see it in her mind,

44

the horror there, the crisped flesh in the ruins,
the children's bodies mangled and contorted,
but she realized her imagination
was the nightly news, where crises must be
so much finite managed information.
She tried to understand how life proceeds
in minute, private gestures burdened with
the knowledge that it's powerless, or if
one gets some small measure of power, it is
only the means to punish, hurt, destroy.
Authority over one's own life alone
is a sick fiction in a world of others.
Three million dead because they could not guide
the will of but a single man and those
scant few who were his loyalist acolytes.
She gestured for another round and laughed
sardonically as tears spilled down her face.
She said that all the talk had made her hungry,
and that she fancied something spicy hot.

FEMALE CHORUS: A woman's victory over love is life
                        apart and singular, dignified and sad.
                        She learns to love the world ferociously.

FEMALE
CHORUS LEADER: When I was small my father told me stories
                        of a girl with a flying white horse who helped
                        all people suffering indignities and pain.
                        She was I, and every night would creep from bed,
                        shout, "Pegasus, Pegasus, Pegasus!" out
                        the window, and the animal appeared
                        to take her on far-flung appointed rounds.
                        My mother was a woman of her time,
                        and found the figure of a female savior
                        amusing, a bit odd, but finally harmless.
                        My dear, wise, shy mother miscalculated
                        the power of my father's sweet enchantments.
                        Oh, father, long-dead, where is my flying horse?
                        Where is my power to help the helpless now?
                        I should hold a single infant to my heart,
                        not to comfort it so much as heal myself.

EAT WHAT YOU KILL

FEMALE
CHORUS LEADER: He touched me as he would something precious.

FEMALE CHORUS: When we go to market, when we shop for meat...

FEMALE
CHORUS LEADER: The hidden cargo of his private voice
was a preternatural contraband.

FEMALE CHORUS: When we go to market, when we shop for meat...

FEMALE
CHORUS LEADER: He made me feel like a special lover.

FEMALE CHORUS: When we go to market,
when we shop for meat,
we squeeze the packages
of creamy bone and tender flesh
and rejoice in our purchasing power.

FEMALE
CHORUS LEADER: But when the heart-shaped catalpa leaves
crisped and fluttered down, he grew secretive,
violent, abstract in his moods, and I wept.

FEMALE CHORUS: Among the clean, delicious aisles of market,
where saccharine music numbs the air, we move
from thing to geometric stack of things,
touching and choosing, touching and choosing.

FEMALE
CHORUS LEADER: He changed so suddenly, he seemed enchanted,
and I, his talisman of ridicule,

became as well the cross he slouched upon
in cathedrals of his waning passion.

FEMALE CHORUS: Produce, canned goods, dairy, deli, frozen things.

FEMALE
CHORUS LEADER: Then the long sorrow, alone and quiet,
memory like the sewing box my mother
rustled through, untangling the delicate threads.
No woman loves her mother more than when
a man has lied and lied, then disappeared.

FEMALE CHORUS: Fresh salmon, the color of a falling sun,
plumbs the hue of hard love's purple bruises,
rich mounds of liver a bovine pudding...

FEMALE
CHORUS LEADER: For weeks I lived on air and good intentions,
lounging in chambers of exquisite hunger,
phone unplugged, the television flickering.

FEMALE CHORUS: In the supermarket death is pretty,
sliced precisely and wrapped in cellophane.

MALE
CHORUS LEADER: In a bar somewhere, I think in Texas,
I fixed upon a neon sign, flashing red,
in which a man riding a bucking bronco
jolted up and off again and again.
For the sake of argument, I'll call the horse
a biological imperative,
the cowboy just another fool in love.

MALE CHORUS: Yippi-yi-ay, another roll in the hay!

MALE
CHORUS LEADER: In the great deserts, nothing is wasted.
I've seen black birds hunched over black carrion
and thought from a distance it looked like love.

MALE CHORUS: Yippi-yi-ay, another roll in the hay!

FEMALE CHORUS: When we go to market, when we shop for meat...

MALE
CHORUS LEADER: Desert nights, something sticks a tongue in my brain,
and for an hour I am passion's prophet.

MALE CHORUS: Yippi-yi-ay, another roll in the hay!

FEMALE
CHORUS LEADER: I have toyed with the notion of difference.
I mean, once, on a summer veranda,
I let a boy touch me everywhere, but laughed
when his earnest gropings turned to tickles.
Then I marvelled how his face colored rose
in the half-light and contorted with shame
at having bungled the chore of arousal.

MALE CHORUS: Yippi-yi-ay, another roll in the hay!

FEMALE
CHORUS LEADER: Yet at some early moment love, the word,
began to simmer at the crowded margins
of each loquacious day, and I could not think
myself a woman but that I would be loved.

FEMALE CHORUS: Through spaces for legs in each silver cart,
                   from the child's seat that folds down, the loose fruit drops
                   to linoleum and rolls down the aisle.

MALE
CHORUS LEADER: Between the word and the meat, the moldering breath
                   and the wet apparatus of its shaping,
                   swoops and glides the carrion will of sex.

FEMALE CHORUS: We have always hated that little seat
                   in supermarket baskets, not because
                   we hate the thing for which it was designed,
                   but for the absence we're reminded of
                   as we pile sweet delicacies upon it.

MALE CHORUS: I laugh and piss off the brink of disaster.

FEMALE
CHORUS LEADER: When I'd grown so hungry I could barely move...

MALE CHORUS: I laugh and piss off the brink of disaster...

FEMALE
CHORUS LEADER: When I was sure I'd starved the thing within me...

MALE CHORUS: I eat what I kill in the wilderness.

FEMALE CHORUS: When I go to market, when I shop for meat...

FEMALE
CHORUS LEADER: When it had seemed to cease to move within me...

MALE
CHORUS LEADER: Ten East from Houston, five AM, the dark
                   spring sky commences a gradual blossoming.
                   The bayou masses gray on either side
                   of a six-lane interstate ruled by trucks.

FEMALE
CHORUS LEADER: When it had seemed to cease to move within...

MALE CHORUS: Trucks hauling chemicals, perishable things,
                   trucks packed with produce, canned goods and meat.

MALE
CHORUS LEADER: In Euripides' *Bacchae,* the brash young king
                   angers the fay god of vegetation,
                   and who doesn't get a little misty-eyed
                   when Mother wakens from her reverie
                   and stares upon the severed head of love?

FEMALE
CHORUS LEADER: I joked of eating for two, and all that first
                   trimester assumed its purblind every need.
                   But then his pretty words stopped feeding me.
                   Romance rotted in his eyes and on his tongue
                   and he philosophized my joy away.
                   Why could he not recall the promises
                   implicit in attentive strokes and glances?
                   Had I become a monster with two heads?
                   I had become a monster with two heads,
                   one weeping constantly, one sequestered in
                   a tangled nest of roots below my heart.

MALE CHORUS: A formal, rank occasion for tender pain,
                   all courtship is a manufactured bliss.

Contrived caresses fix rapacious will,
and all we coo or whisper is a lie.

FEMALE CHORUS: Squatting in the gloom or by a flame,
the squalls and moans of children all around,
the women of the clan await their men
and yearn for bloody meat they may bring back.
The moon is round and high upon a hill,
and things that thrive in darkness howl and click.
One woman grinds dried roots between two stones.
One rocks a dying child before the fire.
One chews a leaf that makes her numb, then dreams
of men who shuffle, chanting, shouldering high
great dripping shanks or red and marbled flesh.

MALE
CHORUS LEADER: As broken lines of causeways stuttered by,
I found a clarity on which my guilt
could stand and castigate my grimmer motives.
I gave her all, then took it back, and fled.

FEMALE
CHORUS LEADER: The earliest stories of what we are
show gods as well as mortals eating children.
I lay before my open bedroom window,
breathing in the rhythm of the soothing breeze,
too weak to move, and wondering if there were
a mechanism by which absorption of
the fetid fist of protein might sustain me.
Such speculation was delirium,
and soon ejection of the thing grown foreign
in death proceeded, and I lay in blood
until a woman friend, guessing my state,
spied thing and me linked as though in carnage,
and jerked me back to weep among the living.
I cannot say the drug of his affection,
taken suddenly away, caused sickness of
an unremittingly convulsive loss.
Withdrawal of affection sucks nothing away,
yet absence of that absence is profound,
and such profundity consumes the will.

I've no idea what I wanted from his love
beyond an affirmation of my life,
one best achieved by work or meditation.
I played the fool, and know myself a fool
to lay my passions bare before a man.

MALE
CHORUS LEADER: Who is more culpable in passion's lie,
he in blind pursuit who perpetrates it,
or she who thrives upon mendacity?

MALE AND
FEMALE CHORUS: In glimmering aisles, all the jars and boxes
vie for our affection, whispering lies,
exaggerating capabilities,
listing all their odious components
in the smallest, least conspicuous print.
Being thus romanced, our thoughts of death subside,
until we reach the rows of packaged meat,
and etherizing Muzak turns grotesque
as artificial air grows rank and chill.

MALE
CHORUS LEADER: Vaguely repentant, even ashamed, I lunged
from one false enthrallment to another,
my affection like a blight of locusts,
though more voracious, quiet, and complete.
Yet when she starved herself to kill the child,
then reported the deed as liberation,
I did not know who or what was free of what
or whom, and cried alone in voiceless dread.

FEMALE
CHORUS LEADER: When I was sure the thing was dead within,
that I myself was but a rasping tomb...

MALE
CHORUS LEADER: The spine-whittling Doppler whoosh of trucks
rumbling west, racing a flashing dawn...

MALE CHORUS:	Praise God of light and limitless spaces.
	Praise God of darkness and imploding stars.
	Praise God of words and their vast dominion.
FEMALE CHORUS:	Our wrath pursues its tail in a dark field.
	Yet we may not wander on a moonless night.
	Alone in open spaces, we are prey.
MALE CHORUS:	Praise God the hunter in the field of light.
	Praise His stealth and patience among stars.
	Praise His true transparent eye and perfect aim.
FEMALE CHORUS:	We did not explode from our father's brow,
	but were constituted from a pool of blood,
	and remain, in essence, a pool of blood.
FEMALE CHORUS LEADER:	When I told him on the phone the thing was dead,
	a quavering buzz of traffic framed his silence,
	and I could only pity him his silence.
MALE CHORUS:	And the brutal father tore half-formed flesh
	from the new charred corpse of its foolish mother,
	then slashed his thigh and stashed the thing inside.
FEMALE CHORUS:	Who does not reckon a fruitful woman
	the measure of renewal and abundance?
	What more fecund image than a woman fat
	with life cruising gleaming aisles of market?
MALE CHORUS:	How passion's carnal play gets reconciled
	with passion's grim directive will define

the gross aesthetic value of our lives
when shelter, food, and leisure are sufficient.

FEMALE
CHORUS LEADER: I am innocent, yet wholly culpable,
and offer no apology or excuse
for self-denial that siphoned off its life.
It was my legal right to purge myself.
The termination was not violent,
was not achieved by artificial means.
The thing began as passionate affection;
an assumption of good faith marshalled it
from that crowded zone of nothingness and bliss.
But tenderness recalled became a hell,
and I, alone yet not alone, contained
the literal essence of a bloody lie.

MALE
CHORUS LEADER: Who can stare upon the sky, night or day,
and not desire to fill the immensity?
I have felt such terror beneath that dome
my hands have trembled and my eyes moistened.
Consider how each star is self-consuming,
how even that rage eight minutes away
is slowly starving towards a grand dispersion.
Shall I now mourn the lolling cinder earth
will be, the inevitable extinction?
I should rather wash my face and change my shirt,
keep my line of vision taut and level,
and move out upon the boulevards of light.
There is much transitory sweetness there.

FEMALE
CHORUS LEADER: I cock the night and hold it to my brain.
I shall remain utterly amazed, or sleep.

54

THE SEARCH PARTY

FEMALE CHORUS:

When surging clouds obliterate the stars,
and no fixed points afford safe passage out
of where the self has led the body's journey,
one hears the fibrillating heart of time.
When the body is lost, completely lost,
the soul retreats into the fear which birthed it.

FEMALE
CHORUS LEADER:

He said two weeks in wilderness would set
him straight, would give midlife a new perspective.
I joked that fourteen days and nights in desert
were better than a string of mistresses,
at least from my perspective as his wife.
So he who rarely in his years had not
awakened to the drone of traffic noise,
a thoughtful man who'd fancied self-reliance
the cultivation of portfolios,
first leased a new Jeep Cherokee, then bought
three-thousand dollars worth of food supplies
and state-of-the-art wilderness clothes and gear,
with which to brave the beasts and elements.
I watched him pack four fifths of premium scotch
and laughed; and he laughed too, then said the nights
get cold, at least he'd read, this time of year.

MALE CHORUS:

Praise the fool that every man will play
as he feels foolish youth bleed out of him.

FEMALE
CHORUS LEADER:

I'm sure he did not know I also saw
him pack among the several books and maps
a Gideon Bible, and Penthouse magazine.

FEMALE CHORUS:

May he who ventures forth into himself
take nothing but the dread that drives him there.

Nine days and nothing of the man himself.
His car and gear neatly encamped below
a sheltering cliff, and every sign he fared
quite well the time that he was there, at least
a week from all that I could see, yet though
we combed a fifty-square-mile radius,
on foot, on horseback, and by helicopter,
we've found no sign of breathing man or corpse.
A dozen times in twenty years I've lead
search parties into shrinking wilderness.
Some fool, or one who's had bad weather luck,
is often losing touch with what sustains him,
stumbling through the brush and hills for days,
dehydrated and hysterical, until
he finds the highway, or by accident
ends where he began, safe among his friends.
But then, every other year or so,
a man gets truly lost, and we are called
to fetch him dead or living from the maw
of truth and beauty, a place that's less a place
than it is a stark condition not of soul,
but what the soul might dream a world to be.
Always, we return with something of the man,
physical proof of his existence there,
a half-dead, sun-burnt, sun-blind, starved and numb
adventurer cleansed of all pretensions,
or a weathered corpse cleansed of all pretensions.
But now nothing, as though the man were nothing,
and a bleached corpse at least is proof of something.
His traceless absence frightens more than death.

MALE CHORUS: Praise the salt each heart releases back to earth.

FEMALE CHORUS: May every heart be vexed by mystery.

MALE CHORUS: Who chances madness chances ecstacy.
Who seeks a vision seeks annihilation.

FEMALE CHORUS: When did the hunt that every man must play,
the going forth and seeking sustenance,
transform from search for food to search for self?
What woman cannot pity him for this?

FEMALE
CHORUS LEADER: I miss him, but subtly, and feel small guilt
that I cannot yet mourn the man whose life
has intersected mine for fifteen years.
A widow needs a corpse by definition.

MALE
CHORUS LEADER: And so we must disband, admit defeat,
for it is for us who know this place defeat
that one as soft, seemingly predictable
as he, could vanish from this space we know
better than ourselves, and we are such as
know ourselves only as we know the space
in which our lives play out apart from others.
But I cannot give up the search for him.
A week, alone, I scour where we had searched
before, and then I check and check again
the cracks and splits in nature like a man
who's lost his keys inside a single room,
but my room is fifty square miles of rock
and brush and redundancies of angles where
a thing of flesh tucked within a crevice
will disassemble down to bone in days.
If I should find his skull lodged between two rocks,
a bit of flesh and clumps of hair still moldering
in patches, I will rejoice as though I'd found
unharmed a missing much-loved child, and kiss
his grin, for what am I while he is lost?

FEMALE CHORUS: How much of history is women waiting?
Sons, fathers, brothers, husbands venture forth
alone or bound together by a purpose.
And so it is that every act that she

performs defines the waiting woman as
a stasis burning through her own blunt will.

We were like sister and brother as much
as married; so intimacy was casual,
if often boring, comforting as well.
We even spoke out honestly of who
among our friends had most attracted us.
Even kinky fantasies we discussed,
not as though confessing as much to boast.
Children have never been an issue; at least
since we discovered he was sterile we
have never felt their absence a fact to mourn.
We were sufficient in our days alone,
rarely argued, avoided pettiness.
I'm surprised how easily I move from room
to room, then door to car to door again.
The rhythm of my life remains the same.
I flip through fifteen years of marriage photos
and laugh or wince at this or that, and feel
familiar warmth, or watch our favorite shows
on television and know what he would say,
or how he would laugh or snicker, yell or sigh
at documentary or nightly news.
Until I see his corpse, he might as well
be visiting his mother for the week
each week that he is absent from my life.

MALE CHORUS: To know the common ground he shares with God
is gender, a man may stand upon the night
and shout commands, and as the words that issue
from his face dissolve into the neutral air,
the sniggering quiet, fatherly and brutal,
signals unconcern brutal and divine.

MALE
CHORUS LEADER: People who sustained themselves upon
this land a thousand years are apparitions;

58

which is to say they're shades of what they were.
Destitute, dependent, fixed to a space
whose borders were determined by invaders,
they sell gross trinkets of their former selves
to tourists randy for old Hollywood's
ideal of rust-skinned naked men who paint
themselves and scream ecstatic as they kill.
The children, always covered with a film
of dust, will play among stripped cars on blocks,
and stop to stare at strangers quietly.
Often I stare back, and do not see enflamed
in large blank irises a wish to know
the glory of their people's history.
Their people have no history, for what
we value in the records of the past
those people fathomed as the cycles of
the lives of everything that moved and breathed.
A son became his father, who was his own
progenitor's best reason for a gentle
death into his own good father's dream of life;
a woman was all women who had lived
to bear new life out of the common will.
The children stare, timeless and out of time,
doomed to enter histories not their own,
in a language foreign, ubiquitous,
and powerless to represent their lives.
I drive backroads, and then the old paths,
then trek the ancient spaces few have known
since conquest of the land by Europeans.
In forbidding hills at sunset I have watched
the land's tenacious vegetation, sparse
and unencumbered one to the next, blaze
then soften into patterns that break one's heart.
In such a landscape every human life
intrudes, and those who came before us knew
this well, and lived in reverent rhythms on
the land, and killed with reverence what sustained them.

MALE CHORUS: He who wills his life apart from others
                    prepares to enter death with dignity.

FEMALE CHORUS: He who lives overwhelmed by thoughts of death
achieves a wisdom that is foolishness,
if joy remains so distant and abstract
the world is soaked in sorrow and distress.

**FEMALE
CHORUS LEADER:**   If he returns, how will his life be changed?
What secret wisdom will his heart contain
and will he speak it unadorned to me?
But I do not require a different man
than he who graced the margins of my life,
passionless, but dependable and safe.
As long as he is absent he's the same,
therefore I must confront the truth of how
I feel secure within uncertainty,
and so admit I wish him gone forever.
Last night, I lay in bed and watched the late show,
burst out laughing so hard I spilled my drink;
I called his name to bring a towel, as though
he'd gotten up to piss or make a sandwich.
It's not that I forgot he wasn't there,
except for just a fraction of a second,
but that I wanted still to hear my voice
pronounce his name throughout the house, to fill
our house with casual yelling of his name.
It sounded natural and appropriate.
So every night I'll yell his name three times—
as though he shuffled in another room—
not loudly in distressful tone, but just
as loud as any lover speaks to ask
a simple favor of one who stands nearby
but out of reach, so close yet out of sight.

FEMALE CHORUS: May she who mourns find antidote for grief.

MALE CHORUS: Praise the lies that make a life worth living.

60

MALE AND
FEMALE CHORUS:
Asleep, each body is beloved, and death,
each lover's profound knowledge of it, is why
it dreams, and why, awake, it dreams of love.

MALE
CHORUS LEADER:
Because we are not intimate with death,
we think romantic love is necessary.
I've spent my life roaming death's great garden,
and know that here all thought is superficial
that does not issue from the nothingness
which is death's only blossom, and so all else
is mere diversion, unworthy of a life
that must be true to all its flinching terrors.
All presence signifies all absence here.
The man I seek now permeates the place.
Each stone and rotting carcass stinks of him,
each cactus needle points to where he stands,
and what there is of liquid here dispersed
through living things or deep beneath the ground,
is blood of him I'll seek until I die.
The man who disappeared without a trace
is trace enough of what I feel divine.
And he is all I need to know of love.

THE DIVORCE

FEMALE CHORUS: Where there are solar systems with two stars,
surely fate of one determines other;
but though one flares much brighter than its mate,
or spins for eons swifter on its pole,
when one must surge, collapse, then throb, then fade,
may other burn alone as though alone?
If one implodes into a pit of darkness
the two are no less coupled than before.
Once coupled, no matter changes that occur
to one or both, two fates are single fate.

MALE CHORUS: Praise desire to become a thing apart.

FEMALE
CHORUS LEADER: Of course it shatters confidence of all
who'd cared for them as something singular.
One couldn't utter name of one and not
also speak of other, as though each were
but residue of other, such that each,
autonomous, distinct, existed yet
to complement the other's graceful life.
So confidence in one's own mating bond
is at least shaken in such times as these
when two, who seemed to cleave so naturally,
without forebodings suddenly must turn
away from expectations and each other.

MALE CHORUS: Praise those who lie alone in beds of grief
because they rose from beds to tell the truth.

MALE
CHORUS LEADER: I think she's touched more deeply by the split
than I, if only for the fact that she
had known them longer as a doting pair.
I never really liked him much, perhaps
because I've never meshed with men who seem

to cultivate their sensitivity
and make a subtle show of tenderness.
I frankly knew that they were doomed when once
I saw him being sensitive with a sad
and gorgeous woman who had sought him out;
indeed, I have no doubt she sought his help.
They occupied a booth behind a window,
and kept their hands around their cups of coffee.
I paused out on the street and just observed
how he tilted his head attentively
and wrinkled up his brow, and frowned, and shook
his head as if in utter disbelief
that any man could hurt a joy like her.
And then, of course, he touched her hand, and then,
of course, he touched her cheek, and I pushed on.
Perhaps he is authentically that way,
perhaps, indeed, no hidden agenda lurked
behind his show of sweetness to that woman.
Perhaps I simply cast my own dark thoughts,
my own lascivious desires onto him.
Perhaps a man can be what he appears.
However, I find him difficult to take
but never must appear to find him so.
Oh, God, I'd love to know he left his wife
for younger stuff, or better yet, a man!

FEMALE CHORUS: Praise her who walks away with dignity.

MALE CHORUS: Praise him who walks away with dignity.

FEMALE AND
MALE CHORUS: False dignity is born of feigned affection.

FEMALE
CHORUS LEADER: He seems quite fond of both, yet not surprised
                       when told by mutual friends the marriage died.
                       I was devastated, shocked silent by
                       the news, in retrospect more deeply moved
                       than such events, in such a world as ours,
                       should reasonably affect in one who's watched
                       a dozen marriages dissolve as through

a microscope one watches mold advance.
As news of their demise—for "they" are dead—
washed over me, I stared across the table
to where he slouched, the candle flicking him,
his crock of bisque steaming in his face.
I wanted him to glance at me, to say
with tender look or grin that we're all right,
that our one life is indivisible.
But he was curious for news of details,
and pressed our friends to talk out all the dirt.
Was one, were both, involved with someone else?
Was he a cheating bastard in sheep's clothing?
Did she or he initiate the break?
I knew our marriage bond was unto death.
I knew that though he lives distracted, hunched
within himself, he must have me for light,
for those occasions when he crawls outside
himself and, squinting, sniffs the air and stretches,
then roams about through stiff congenial gossip.
He must have me to charm the world he loathes
but cannot manage to avoid, and I
can play the part of cheery antidote
to his dyspeptic gloom so well that some
are simply moved by starkness of the contrast.
We've been a hit for years among our friends,
or, rather, the friendships I sustained in spite
of him, the friendships that he tolerates.

MALE CHORUS: Praise gray sustaining solitary moods
in midst of those few others who reveal,
with subtle gestures, subtle ruthlessness.
Praise impulse to recede within a state
of insincere congeniality.

MALE
CHORUS LEADER: I actually found her mildly interesting,
quite attractive, and once enjoyed a talk
we had at some pretentious dinner party
where he held forth, tastefully of course, about
a poor endangered species in a place
whose name seemed not to have a vowel, and where
the local custom was to eat the thing

exclusively each day of rainy season.
We spoke of recipes for cog she'd read
translated from Chinese, and laughed out loud
when fluffy yappers of our host went off
at small disturbances in neighbors' yards.
So then I sensed the fissure in their lives,
their temperaments, the ways they viewed the world.

FEMALE CHORUS: Behold the silent signal of distress.

MALE
CHORUS LEADER: And wondered if she found appealing such
a man as I who views sardonically
the vast corrosive world of otherness,
for surely living in the shadow of
a saint, as I do too, for her must be
as stifling as a cloister on a hill,
a place whose verve pale piety has sapped.
Similar to me, she seems addicted
to his goodness, to how the world is drawn
to him and calmed by all he thinks and says,
as though it seems to others that if one
so dedicated to a decent life
of utterly engaged transparency
can live among them, surely their own sins
of quaint duplicity might be diminished.
I glanced across the room at my own mate,
my graceful, quiet, good and decent wife,
and caught her earnestly engaged in talk
with my poor interlocutor's good man.
Their brows seemed stitched with furrowed flags of deep
concern for whales and starving children, soil
erosion, baby seals, and global warming,
and so it seemed their heads prepared to sail
heroically away upon their vast
tumultuous ocean of regard for others.
And there we stood, addicted to their goodness,
ironical, conflicted, paralyzed,
just watching, always watching from the shore.

FEMALE CHORUS: Beware deflected discourses of rage,
the white flame beneath the cool black lid
of irony and languid indirection.

MALE CHORUS: Praise passions that are stripped and pummeled blossoms.
Praise all debilitating promises.
Praise loathing that is pure and kin to love.

FEMALE
CHORUS LEADER: He's always been there for me, or for himself,
perhaps, though for my sake at least in terms
of ignorant effect, for I've assumed
him faithful keeper of my secret life,
a taciturn yet noble lover of
the truth of what I am and seek to be,
and I until the troubling breach have stood
transparent in my every word to him.
Yet now I peer into the man I've loved
and cannot see beyond his surface; it seems
that tiny mirrors hang all over him,
and black oil pools the spaces in between.
There is no revelation in this life
as when the most familiar thing one knows
becomes with stunning suddenness more foreign
than quantum weirdness to an average mind.
I wonder if it was that way with her,
though likelier I think that she transformed
to his more trusting eyes, becoming one
not cruel, unfaithful, tactless or malign,
but shattered at the core such that to lift
her like a doll and shake would be to hear
a thousand tiny shards rattling like rice,
or filaments of plastic trapped within.
And yet it seems now that the world divides
this way, between the solid and the shattered,
between the guileless lover and beguiled
beloved, and usually one will find
the other, though happiness is possible
for either only with its own kind near:

a shattered core should find a shattered core,
and solid one to solid one is bliss.
lover to lover, beloved to itself...

FEMALE CHORUS:

Beware all revelations of the heart,
for hearts are protean and self-consuming.

MALE CHORUS:

Praise the protean nature of the heart,
and praise how hearts may clear their own debris.

MALE
CHORUS LEADER:

One time, when we were young, I held her tight
in the middle of a crowd, New Years, I think,
or Independence Day; I can't recall
if we were dressed for chill or summer warmth,
nor even can I conjure if we stood
upon a city square, or golf-course green
beneath the booming blooms of fireworks.
I only know that moment I was moved
by her proximity to glimpse my death,
and at that moment we were bound together.
The question, the question that defines my life
now that it soaks each moment in its passing,
is whether our untethering would be
a glimpse of life, of what is possible
in time so brief, or whether it would seem
a diminution I would suffer yet
unto myself, unto eternity.

FEMALE
CHORUS LEADER:

Divorce by definition is to turn
away, and so by etymology
we are, perhaps, divorced, and have been for
so many years I'm frightened to recall
if there was a moment it occurred,
a fixed point in our lives I might remember.
I do recall the moment he was mine.
We'd strolled out to the pier one autumn night
when city fathers had decided to

display our civic pride back to ourselves.
It was the anniversary of when
some klutz in eighteen eighty-something signed
the charter that our hometown issued from,
and pyrotechnics lit the sky, as one
young man held one young woman and shivered there
beneath the stars and blue and golden blooms,
amid the slack-jawed neighbors of their youth.
I saw then in his eyes that I was his,
and realize now our lives are mortgaged to
our first enchantment, and that we've finally paid
the last installment, and only now may say
we own outright the life each lost to it.

FEMALE CHORUS: Praise solitary life in middle years.

MALE CHORUS: Beware unclasping lives in middle years.

FEMALE AND
MALE CHORUS: There is never freedom from the other.
The other is a presence unto death.
It is the gesture of rejection where
resides the radical new life one seeks,
and it is fleeting yet sustaining as
a new fixed point from which to leave the world.

MALE
CHORUS LEADER: I'm paralyzed to act upon desire.

FEMALE
CHORUS LEADER: Released unto myself, I'll walk away,
and though I'll drag his essence after me,
I'll make of it a thing to stash inside
a box and place up high upon a shelf.

THE SCENT

FEMALE CHORUS: Anonymity among the sovereign shades
requires the stealth of one in love with shades.

MALE CHORUS: The secret act of passion is a coin
to spend against the terror of the grave.
It buys a momentary, lavish hush
of fear, diminishing the debt of peeved
and anxious life to that alternative
to life which is the bane of consciousness.

FEMALE CHORUS: Praise all who lie for secret passion's sake.

MALE CHORUS: The promise of eternal bliss must break
upon the winding wheel of finite days.

FEMALE
CHORUS LEADER: His presence I define against his absence,
and he is absent more than he is here,
as I am always here, and, so, a place
to which he may retreat at his convenience.
A woman's secret married lover lies
to her advantage, if advantage means
his presence in her life from time to time.
And it is not his wife alone who cleaves
his private from his public self such that
I am compelled to live, for love of him,
within a deeper realm than privacy.
With her he lives a private life; with me
he lives a secret one, and difference
resides in what his lies enable him
to be in public life: a man who loves
his mate and children publicly earns trust,
and trust is money, money power, and power

is some of what I love in him, and so
have tolerated absence as condition
of his occasional presence in my life.

FEMALE CHORUS: Praise lonely women's love of men who steer
upon the winds of violent passages.
Praise the vital presence of her who waits,
for by her patience she defines his journey.

MALE CHORUS: Beware the secret joys that hatch delusions.

MALE
CHORUS LEADER: My little girl was once my little girl.
She will indulge my doting old man's love
unto my death, my old man's touch,
or late-night call to see if she is well.
My only daughter, born of only wife
a year now underground, is mourning not
for mother gone, or youth that seeps away,
but for the absence of a living man.

FEMALE CHORUS: Praise tenderness of him who tends the garden.
Praise simple intentions of the gardener.

MALE
CHORUS LEADER: When she was four she broke her chin upon
a wicked wooden edge of something in
the house; I pressed a chunk of ice upon
her wound as she howled against the pain and blood.
I held her in my arms; her mother drove.
The doctor sewed her up and we went home.
That night she asked if devils eat small children.
I told her devils don't exist, but if
they did they'd only eat the waking ones.
Last week I saw her eyes were bloodshot, sunken,
but did not ask about her nights, if all
her waking hours through the morning gloom
were haunted by a demon in her heart.

I simply touched her face, ran my thumb
across the little scar beneath her chin.

The ponderous moon, prodigal and moot,
may signify the clumsy longings of
a desperate woman who knows not to give
her better self to one beyond her touch.

Praise the dead moon's dark and secret side.
Praise hidden acts of all who seek distraction
from ordinary terrors of their lives.

I'll not become the clinging shrew, the wronged
and vengeful crazy other woman bent
on smashing all I cannot have completely.
I've barely too much dignity for that.
Though twice I've stooped to spying on his wife,
and found her sweet and dignified, if thick
across the waist and double-chinned, a bit
too happy with her quaint and busy life.
I watched her scoop her children up from school
and dance them through a slick suburban mall.
Her teenaged girls addressed her as a friend,
and I admired the ease with which she spoke
to them about the details of their days.
I could not help but like her, and yet could see
how he whose life is tied to hers might wish
to slip away from all that sunshine, all
that perky, chubby, shallow happiness.
Because true passion sometimes needs a darkness,
a man in middle years may comb the shadows.
I am the shadow in his life, the dark
place he requires from time to time to time.
I cannot blame him for my agitation.
He never lied about his family life.
And yet the power of his will upon
my life, the quiet conflagration of
my private life he should account for, as I
account for every hour of sleep I lose.

FEMALE CHORUS: The dawn ignites the branches and the leaves,
and every tiny singer is a phoenix
for a moment; for a moment every
sleepless lover blazes at her window.

MALE
CHORUS LEADER: When she was nine and ten I smelled some nights
of something that her mother never wore,
a scent not subtle or ambiguous.
I did not even try to mask it, did
not care much what her mother thought or said,
though she said nothing, acting eerily
as if she thought my infidelity,
all classic signs of which were obvious,
was but a necessary stage of marriage.
My baby, her smile a silver grid, her arms
so skinny they seemed but strings around my neck,
would jump into my arms each night and squeal
her joy, chattering in bursts about her day.

FEMALE CHORUS: A candle swears itself a raging star;
such is the constancy of lovers' oaths.

MALE CHORUS: Praise passion's whispered promises and oaths.

FEMALE CHORUS: Beware the promises of feverish love.

FEMALE
CHORUS LEADER: The revelation of his decency
occurred the night we worked into the dawn
to meet a deadline that was life or death,
in business terms, for quarterly reports.
He would not fudge the numbers, though the way
to do so with impunity was clear,
and so he sacrificed a sure advancement
to a bureaucratic point of honor.
It's maybe not the stuff of action movies,

but still a victory over pettiness.
And I congratulated him, and asked
him over for a drink, a small collegial
gesture with no salacious overtones.
We drank some wine, and talked, and laughed, and then
he left, politely, and the weeks peeled by.
At work we often took our breaks together,
and then we lunched, and then had drinks at dusk.
A friendship grew; he often asked advice
about his girls, and did not hide affection
for his wife. His nature is to simplify,
yet with each day of casual contact I
grew complicated in my feelings for him.
Such complex little knots of feeling surfaced,
a floating knotted rope whose other end
was tethered to a hulk that lay deep down,
the wreckage of compulsions from a time
I could not frame or calculate as time.
I told him, suddenly, we could not meet
away from office work, and gave no reason.
He called. We talked. I emphasized desire
to be alone a while, for private reasons.
He called again, came over for a drink,
and I again made clear I wanted quiet.
Then one night he appeared without announcement,
and said quite simply that he missed our friendship,
and so I told him I could not be his friend.

MALE CHORUS: Praise all men who live with good intentions.

FEMALE CHORUS: Beware all men's sincerity in love
                      when such sincerity is power's issue.

FEMALE
CHORUS LEADER: His power over others is his pure
                      affection for the simple truths in life.
                      He'll rise to prominence on his own terms
                      within the company, a trusted man.
                      He bears but one mendacity, and I
                      am that one secret decency endures.
                      I am endured, merely, for passion's sake.

My bitter heart endures his decency
less well each sleepless night, and I grow strong,
by small degrees, against the gross compulsions
I cannot name, or conjure out of time.

MALE CHORUS:

Praise not the lives of decent men too much.
At each one's core is passion's prohibition.
Praise rather him who lives without pretense.

FEMALE CHORUS:

Praise always him who lives without pretense.

MALE
CHORUS LEADER:

My little girl could smell perfume of her
whose selfless love I sought at my convenience.
I reeked of it each time I left the bed
that woman offered me without conditions.
It's said olfactory is powerful
beyond the other senses, and memories
that lay the deepest are revived by it.
So when, the other day, I rang the door,
holding blossoms to cheer my daughter, the scent
was slight until she opened, and then it blew
across the half of life I'd squandered in
a loveless marriage to a decent woman,
a dull alliance for our child's sole sake.

MALE CHORUS:

Praise wasted lives of all who sacrifice.

FEMALE
CHORUS LEADER:

I never understood why a woman wears
a scent so strong it dominates a room,
but when I passed one of those annoying girls
who's paid to roam a store and spray the shoppers,
I was enchanted by a cheap Parisian
imitation I recognized as one
I once associated with a sweetness,
a comforting, though that is all I know.
Particulars elude me. I can't recall

occasion or the source of sweetest comfort.
But now I spray the scent upon my body,
and live within its vague associations.

FEMALE CHORUS: Praise consolations that are small but true.

MALE CHORUS: Praise consolations that are small but true.

FEMALE
CHORUS LEADER: My father's flowers wither in a vase.

A TERRIBLE SECRET

FEMALE CHORUS: Inside each word that guilty men may speak,
no matter if they broach their lives in truth
or comment casually upon the weather,
a ravenous worm will gnaw the substance down
to milky pulp, dissolving delicate webs
attaching thing to word, and word to breath.

MALE CHORUS: There are crimes redemption will not speak to bless.
One man may murder hideously then change
into a saint, another choose to be
a silent witness of banal deceit
and never speak away that petty lie,
roiling in his secret unto sleep.

FEMALE
CHORUS LEADER: To clear him for this work they probed his past
such that my own past youthful escapades
appeared in bureaucratic language stuffed
in files our eyes should never wish to scan.
Indeed, a top official hinted that
my life before him almost shut him out
of necessary clearance for this work.
"This work" I say, yet don't know what it is
except that governments most everywhere
by turns must fear and covet what it does.
His work involves, though, process less than thing,
at least he seems to hint that this is true.
Yet even so he will admit he lies,
is told to lie to me, when speaking in
the vaguest terms regarding what he does.
So my darling mate is most sincere about
mendacities his work requires, and I
must never press regarding what it is.
His work and life are bonded seamlessly,
but I can feel the join, a minute fold,
a psychic hair-line fissure where his work
and he form boundaries, such as magnets make
to lodestone bars with which they mate and breed

invisible dynamic fields of current.
His essence I must never know is field
of such a current, invisible exchange
of charge and valence such that one is both
as they are joined, and they are joined forever.

FEMALE CHORUS: What is this that holds all life in balance?

MALE CHORUS: What new abomination steers our fates?

FEMALE AND
MALE CHORUS: What elegant system breeds our new despair?

MALE
CHORUS LEADER: They come at dawn as inconspicuous cars:
tastefully expensive, windows tinted,
neutral colors, quiet, almost serene.
They flash their passes, and I must check each name
against the roster, run my wand across
the bar code on each card though each face smiles
familiar from its half-receded window.
Past me, each one, I'm told, must shuffle through
three more degrees of stiff security
before the morning gossip over coffee,
before the narratives of last night's game,
before the hunkering down to secret work.

FEMALE CHORUS: What place is this where some find joy in sorrow?

FEMALE
CHORUS LEADER: Some days, mid-morning, after he is there
a while, I park a distance from the gate
and gaze past where the man identifies
the bodies sanctioned for that world he guards.
He sits inside his booth, and gazes off,
it seems, though probably he gazes at
a screen, a monitor on which I show.
There is one way in, which is the one way out.
He knows no more of what my husband does

within than I, and like me takes on faith
that he is not accomplice to a crime
of such proportion weeping is absurd.
The fence is high, electrified, and barbed.
The rumors are that landmines lay within,
and that atop each massive, windowless hulk
of blue-gray concrete soldiers shoulder missiles.
The guard has strapped upon his hip a gun,
a funny, useless little gun with which
to scare himself at night, perhaps, when all
are sleeping in his house, and he is drunk.

MALE CHORUS:　　　Praise all whose empty lives are duty-bound.

FEMALE CHORUS:　　Praise all who seek redemption in their work.

MALE AND
FEMALE CHORUS:　　Praise all whose empty work redeems their lives.

MALE
CHORUS LEADER:　　She's beautiful and weird, a manikin
inside her car, though, soon, she pours out
and leans back on the hood and freezes there
regarding some fixed point inside the fence.
Of course I've checked her out and know whose wife
she is, whose overwhelmed and puzzled mate.
The boys in deep security stop short
of saying she is nuts, though hint that years
ago, before the marriage, she was wild.
By this of course they mean promiscuous,
and they know almost everything about
the spouses, parents, friends and children of
these men and women bound to secret work.
Why does she come? What is she looking for?
Does he whose life is tied to hers know she
comes here to spy, through wire, on grass and gray
cement, or is he too consumed to care?

FEMALE CHORUS: Forgive the necessary secrets some
who love define their silent passion by.

FEMALE
CHORUS LEADER: Sometimes, while staring at those massive boxes,
I wonder not so much at what they hold,
as what dark principle must organize
free wills to bleak tasks with such cheer as they
within must fabricate from week to week.
Rumors fly, but no one really knows
what poisoned stuff they cook within those walls.
Sometimes I see what in the distance looks
like bee keepers, in bleached-white baggy suits
and massive masks, trot from the farthest box
through little doors onto, it seems, a path
into the ground, for each one disappears,
it seems from half a mile, into the ground.

MALE CHORUS: Praise witnesses to secret rituals.

FEMALE
CHORUS LEADER: If only I could tell him how his life
of secret work has liberated me,
how though I play the vexed yet pliant mate
my shame, my secret shame, which is my soul,
I may keep hidden with impunity,
and hidden, coterminous with his, it is
a kind of warped, benign, and coreless joy.
As he was moved in courtship to reveal
every secret of his life but of his work,
so I confessed to every tryst and fancy
but that which ripped my innocence apart.

FEMALE CHORUS: Praise her who hides her shame with dignity.

MALE
CHORUS LEADER: Is longing all that brings her here to gaze?
Is this which seems to me a mystery

to fear, to her a citadel of passion?
One time at Kelly's Bar a guy who works inside
got smashed and blathered on of children dead.
A colleague, lucid by comparison,
strong-armed him out the door to God-knows where,
for never again his face rolled through the gate
to work, or into Kelly's Bar to drink.
I love my country as I love my life,
and so it is mid-life's self-loathing, born
of fear, compels a secret loathing—of
my country—born itself of fear.
What pattern does she see that I am blind to?
Does his official life so titillate?
Is she aroused by secrets for the sake
of secrets, or is her gaze an angry glare?
Is what I see as passion hot contempt?
I guard an entrance to a place where hell
is brewed, and yet I don't know what it is
I guard, for hell is relative and boring.
It could be wicked bliss, a death in life
ecstatic, outside time, or suffering
unambiguous, frank, and unabashed.

MALE CHORUS:

The pall, the sick sweet pall of sunset on
cathedrals chills regard and pools remorse.

FEMALE CHORUS:

Whose life is life in wake of violation?

FEMALE
CHORUS LEADER:

I told my sister everything, and she
entrusted me—I thought—with all she felt.
When girlish passions rose like mercury
to flush my cheeks and tear my eyes at night
she stroked my hair and did not say a word.
And yet that edifice of trust would crumble.
One night I witnessed what the sound of which
had numerous times, perhaps for years, wavered
above my deepest sleep like Northern Lights.
No word or image surfaced to my shocked
regard, and fear of alien presence I
assumed until that moment cool, familiar,

a source of succor if not affection, blazed
in my imagination like a demon.
Yet after that I thought I hated her.
She lived in hell and would not take me there,
would not confide her pain and weep with me.
My sister's secret was my secret from
that moment on, and all that we had felt,
I'd thought as one, became a quiet lie.

FEMALE CHORUS: Praise the courage of the silent victim.
                   Praise the witness of the victim's outrage.

MALE CHORUS: Praise confessions that deploy hot malice.

MALE
CHORUS LEADER: Depending on the season, the cars file out
                   even as or after sunset dumps its smog-
                   intensified bright gloss upon the edge
                   of day, and I go home, or to a bar,
                   as my relief begins to wave the night
                   shift in and bad dogs bark at distant check points.
                   Efficiency is always beautiful
                   when evil enterprises are concealed.
                   The pure reductive artifice of function
                   requires the quarrel with nature be refined
                   down to a few delicate gestures of
                   dismissal, as a master to a slave.
                   Secrets are the essence of all passion,
                   intimacy, artifice, and evil.
                   My silly little job, more show than real,
                   allows at least a constant state of wonder.
                   The rumors lost their luster long ago,
                   and I am through much caring what dark task
                   so organizes human wills like this.
                   I stride out to the parking lot and pause
                   as night lights snap their glare across the field
                   of giant bunkers; false pride, ironic
                   to its core yet sentimental still, fills
                   my numb conflicted heart, and I must marvel
                   at my own complicity with evil.
                   For I, privy to nothing, guard the gate.

THE PLAYER

MALE CHORUS:

In ages past, great crowds collected on
the hills surrounding battle fields, as men
would break in waves upon advancing foes.
The noise of killing wound with that of dying
appeared to all an ecstasy of life
intense beyond concerns that drove it forward.
What greater awe is there than what he feels
who stands so safe upon a rise to know
the mortal print of rage against despair,
the writhing hierogliphs of distant battle?

MALE
CHORUS LEADER:

His story is the classic one: she clung
to him of her own will, and what she said
and how she spoke, demurred, and glanced
away then back meant that she wanted him.
They drank and touched and slipped away from all
the other players and their dates, and when
he pressed she resisted only for the show.
She wanted him like every other girl
at school, and so he took what wanted taking.

FEMALE CHORUS:

We are civilized so long as bodies may
determine sovereign borders as do nations.
And like a nation, every body must
assume its borders clear and sacrosanct.

MALE
CHORUS LEADER:

But God, the kid is great. He has the eyes,
the arm, the feet, the heart, the head, the hands
to carry mediocrity to heights
beyond its true collective will and power.
He is a warrior, born to battle odds
and bleak contingencies and cram the world
down every sissy cynic's throat and laugh.
The game must dream one such as he every
generation, and I have dreamed of coaching

a freak, a gorgeous monster such as he,
of fathering such a hero to the game.

FEMALE
CHORUS LEADER: I know her type, and am repulsed by all
she represents: her daddy's money, galas
where children of the rich are paired to breed,
her pill-numbed mother's charities, and each
relentless fashion signifying space
between the wealthy and the rest of us.
I took her deposition, probed her will
and memory, made her stare into the shame,
reveal to me the details of her most
humiliating, haunted recollections.
And I believe her every word. I doubt
neither what she meant by resisting him
nor what he thought she meant. She is a fool
protected by the wisdom of the law,
the law which states no will to dominate
may ever act by force upon the weak.
But she is weak now only in the flesh.
Her money is her righteous angel of
revenge, and he, a hero to the town
until her accusation of the act,
is now the beast incarnate to all eyes.

FEMALE CHORUS: When gods descend for sport and pleasure we
whom they seek may shun advances, flee, or fight.
Divine passion is inexorable, though,
and we who are its objects lose our selves
within it, shattered ships inside the storm.

MALE CHORUS: To lose one's self within a dangerous act,
to feel and see, to move and be the act
is death in life, is ecstasy, is war.

MALE
CHORUS LEADER: He is unselfconscious, an animal
wholly unconcerned with its own beauty,
and though his boyish bloated ego grates
upon mature regard, when he is on

the field, or waiting, patient, on the sideline,
he is oddly quiet, even humble,
maybe even reverent towards the game.
It is always true that great ones never lose
their sense of awe within the play of process,
the game itself indeed is ritual
to them, a mutable cathedral where
each prayer is execution of a role.

FEMALE CHORUS: When no is no, is never yes, is no.

FEMALE
CHORUS LEADER: He turns brutality into a dance,
a free-form celebration of a pattern,
whatever play contingency declares.
What joyous life one such as he must know
when who he is is only what he does.
I've watched him as a female fan may see,
without vicarious motives, without desire
to be that thing, that animal, that man
performing as if every victory
were secondary motive to destruction
of each opponent's will to masculine pride.
I watch him as I watch the falling sun
spill its brutal blaze upon horizon.
So what is she whose dignity requires
extinguishing a mortal power: a source
of mortal wonder, or receptacle
of fantasies and dreams of pure transcendence?
I look at her and see a woman wronged,
and no less so than if he'd broken down
her door then held a blade against her throat.
My sympathy for him and loathing of her
I feel against a primal sense of duty
to women everywhere and for all time.
But God, the kid can throw the ball a mile!

FEMALE CHORUS: When no is no, is never yes, is no.

MALE CHORUS:

The blood of something dead a while is black,
or nearly so in certain fields of light.
The quiet after carnage is a pool
of oil that soaks into the dirt and sky.

MALE
CHORUS LEADER:

I saw him first play ball in junior league,
a city scheme to keep kids off the streets.
He was a stick with sticks for arms and legs
so long and slim they seemed to live apart,
in cooperation with the rest of him
yet somehow free unto themselves to act.
It always seems that greats discover how
their greatness is a matter of a will
quite other than the one that bears their names,
the self-aware and self-regarding core
of each identity must dance desire
with its own body's will, a force apart
and foreign to all but athletes and heroes.
He cannot spell his name without a crib,
yet what delicacy in the midst of brute
kinetic blur of hurling bodies he
exhibits, what precision and finesse,
and what a sense of timing and nuance,
even—with a lead—a sense of irony,
all qualities we affix to genius.

MALE CHORUS:

Praise those who laugh at death and do not turn
or hesitate when faced with harm and loathing.
Praise those who do not live to die yet face
impending dreadful odds of failure smiling.

FEMALE CHORUS:

Praise her who simply speaks a simple truth.

FEMALE
CHORUS LEADER:

Expensive clothes, ridiculous perfect hair
puffed and tinted, make-up meticulous,
she sat, hands folded on her offended lap.

She said she'd really thought that he was nice,
and therefore trusted him completely when
he said a walk across the beach would clear
his head of alcohol, and she should come.
I realized then what expectations coiled
within her quaint conception of the "nice."
It held at center point heroic sense;
one dubbed so could not lie about intentions,
was pure and chivalric beyond reproach,
and I wondered how such trust could incubate
within one born as I unto this world,
this world where every indication is
that women suffer for their trust in men.
And therefore I trust none in courtship, where what
I am is all I am in terms of sex,
though in my job I wear my duty like
a badge that covers what I am by nature
that I may recreate the essence of
what private life does not allow to charm.
What I am is human female, but who
I am I am still determining, and shall
continue fashioning unto my death.
Let no man think biology is all
there is of me, nor of himself; for as
the tides of passion shift, retreat, and swell
to shift again, recede, and swell once more,
a star implodes for every heartbreak, a star
collapses at the core of all our own
names have meant to us when we lie awake
and intensely alone, and gender is dragged
into that jet inward rushing, that dark
much darker than utter black, that crushed light.

MALE CHORUS: Praise the man of action who does not love.

FEMALE CHORUS: Praise the hearts of cowards who cannot love.

MALE CHORUS: Praise men who love the world and hate themselves.

FEMALE CHORUS:	Praise all who live to change the world for love.
MALE CHORUS:	Praise fools who live to love and change the world.
FEMALE CHORUS:	Praise fools who live to love and change the world.
FEMALE AND MALE CHORUS:	Praise fools who live to love and change the world.
FEMALE CHORUS:	Praise fools...
MALE CHORUS:	Praise fools...
FEMALE CHORUS:	Praise fools...
MALE CHORUS:	Praise fools...
FEMALE CHORUS:	Praise fools...
FEMALE AND MALE CHORUS:	Praise fools...
FEMALE CHORUS LEADER:	I am bored with weeping victims, and bored with talk of how to change the world with love. There is no love, only coalitions for survival, predators and victims dancing, exchanging roles from time to time.

The old and huge ideas are overwhelmed.
We live determined by conceptions of
heroic being, and yet the world requires
rank selflessness for mutual survival.
And so we inch along the razor's edge
of slow extinction, naming the bloody route
transcendence, the process such sweet mystery.
The golden boy is what we really are
when dreams are peeled away and life revealed:
a knack, a glorious knack for getting by
from second to second, for surviving
second by second the rush of nature,
the only enemy, the only foe
worthy of our conscious retribution.
He is in and out of nature all at once,
and so are all the rest of us, though not
as comfortably so as those few freaks who love
the world through love of danger, and launch from each
lived moment a mindless intensity.
He is so absurd he touches the divine,
and as such is a danger to us all,
for touching pure transcendence he transforms
relations both in nature and without,
and there is no outside of nature but
within absurd and mindless games we lose
our lives to for a little while as if
to die, and in that death forget we die.
A girl no less absurd than he is hurt.
Her pain is real and will not fade from thought.
All human law must be a force of nature.

BROTHER LOVE

CHORUS
(MALE AND FEMALE):   The fibrillations of a man's sorrow,
brief consequence of terror in self-knowledge,
presage a bottomless plunge towards solitude.
Perhaps he cries for all the pain he's caused.
Perhaps he curls up in the dark and sobs.
Perhaps he presses death between his eyes
and squeezes off his one unselfish act.
But each lucky man has one brother in pain,
his life lived otherwise, or parallel.

GAY BROTHER: I have done one terrible thing. I was born.
I have performed one great act many times.

STRAIGHT BROTHER: To think the same woman gave breath to us,
the same man coaxed us from the permutations
of his marvelous body's difficult code.

GAY BROTHER: In those woods behind our uncle's house
a path as narrow as a boy's quick stride
burned serpentine through brush to the black stream.

CHORUS: Praise innocent journeys on summer days.

GAY BROTHER: By the fallen enormous trunk of oak
that breached the breadth of the small water's flow,
I found a dirty piece of cloth, some boy's
shed briefs he'd tossed aside before plunging in.

CHORUS: Praise sweet guilt of confused awakenings.

STRAIGHT BROTHER: I think I knew his body's revelation.
I think I knew the day he found his path.

GAY BROTHER: I plucked it up, and brushed it off, and held
it to my cheek, and felt a sobbing rage
rush through my groin, and realized friendship meant
to me a thing, an act, a symmetry
that other boys would fear and wish to kill.

STRAIGHT BROTHER: Fraternal twins, our raw coterminous fates
distinct at birth but mutually determined,
we grew into an intimate self-loathing
indicative of primal brother love.

CHORUS: At inception, God the baby wept and wailed
to conjure forth a flash and silver surface,
and seeing that It was a lovely God,
cooed itself a sphere of machinations,
of whirling contradictions signifying
each to each the essence of necessity.

STRAIGHT BROTHER: We lay in separate beds and whispered dreams
and lies and boasted, as our father did,
that we would have the world for ransoming.
He was my passionate foe and confidant.
When we touched, it was for brutal pleasure,
wrestling on the fragrant morning grass.

CHORUS: Praise the angular beauty of the day.
Praise the frank inconstant stars and summer skies.
Praise the stiffening contours of the night.

STRAIGHT BROTHER: But then it seemed a sentimental pall
of adolescent doom covered him in smoke,
and he stepped forth another than I had known.
He read of chivalric lives—always soft,
fair and verdant— idyllic nobility,
as though on the plane of fiction and dreams,
where nothing shits nor flies insult the air,
his rooting, squealing new desire might sleep.
I did not have the heart for what he was,
and just the faintest concept of the laws
of nature his abominations cursed.
Several humid nights I followed him to town
and observed him lounging on a gaslit stoop
until a fatherly car would slow, open,
and brother of my flesh would pause, then enter.
Shocked, unfamiliar with the symptoms of grief,
I strangled soft affection for his name.

CHORUS: He who awakens to his mortal difference,
he who is changed and suffers change, will plunge
into Death's tangled currents and emerge
gasping, dripping mortality, coughing prayers.

GAY BROTHER: First I was darling of the dirty secrets,
the cloistered fancy of the timid butch.
"Just think of me as your special daddy,"
one pink-skinned, balding Volvo told me.
Later, I found a crayon on the seat
in back, and slipped it in my pocket with
the bills he slipped me before he sped away.
But I wanted love, not old men's money.
I wanted a special friend, like a brother,
only more intimate, rough yet tender.

CHORUS: The burning issues on the tongues of angels
are heaven's forfeitures of reasoned mercy.

When God pontificates, the speed of light
is that at which the throngs of blessed ones pass
from bliss to boredom, to nodding somnolence.

GAY BROTHER: Romantic, pale, hazed light of surrender,
the whole round thing stopped the night like a cork.
A starry effervescence seemed to hiss
with joy I heard but could not see, face-down
as I was in grass, my lover's fingers wound
through my hair as though I galloped in the dark.

STRAIGHT BROTHER: I gazed over the rim of a stinking can,
not twenty yards from where a writhing flower
shed violent silhouettes across the brink
of shrubs and stones that lined the river bank.
What churning pain was this that he called love?
What rank humiliation drove his needs?
Persecution halted with terminal grunts.
The agent of pain backed out like a cat,
drew up the denim gathered at his ankles,
sniffed and smirked at the indolent moon, then strolled
towards spangled city streets, smoothing his hair.
My brother lifted to his elbows, then knees,
his face pouring down like a snapped blossom.

CHORUS: Deep zones of mystery are passing away.
Great healing jungles are aching with flames.
The waters are choking. Skies dissipate.
Who, seeking love, should wish procreation?

STRAIGHT BROTHER: He beat us for the sake of filial love,
a father's proud desire that sons should be
the living monuments of how he lived.
There was of course a ritual to it all.
Feeling left his face like draining liquid,
and he stood as still as God the longest moment,

92

until he slowly pointed to the hook
where his razor strap would droop like bacon.
The offender's part was to fetch it to him
then lay across the couch arm, mute supplicant,
pants down. But he would sometimes make us wait.
Often a sweaty minute, one time with me
an hour before he lashed my flesh five times
ferociously. The pain would burn for days.
But once, I don't know why, my brother lay
bare-assed across the couch arm for an hour,
then another, until the house grew dark
and still he did not move nor father come
to lash him for some boyish indiscretion.
That morning I awakened to his weeping,
and when I peered across the banister
I saw him still arched over, fouled and wet,
sobbing for forgiveness, begging for pain.

CHORUS:

When angels mourn, the lamps grow dim in nurseries,
and newborns paw the air and cast blurred eyes
upon dark ceilings, where the new dead float.
The infants, whose brief souls are angel's tears,
are so pristine the blessed can but weep the more,
though new dead grumble for a quick revenge
on those who weep to weep that perfect soul
whose nature is the slide to such corruption
as they, being dead, escaped yet yearn for still.

GAY BROTHER:

That world I found within the world was true
to those shrill longings chanting in my blood.
When acrimony of my father's voice
intensified beyond what I could bear,
when the world outside my world had choked with shame
for what by nature, or unnatural design—
the difference to my heart is only words—
my body's separate will had shunned convention,
I orphaned my soul, speculation's breath,
unto the living city's lap of danger,
where no mother's sighs, father's rage, brother's shock
could burst exquisite dreams of satisfaction.

CHORUS: Praise the blank wall where many families weep
               a sorrow greater than the world's blue turning.
               Praise the falling fist and the flinching brow.

STRAIGHT BROTHER: These twenty years since I twice saw him so,
               deranged and glowing with humiliation,
               my righteousness has softened for the wisdom
               that I have since curled over for a few
               no less inglorious humiliations,
               and if he remains a mortal mystery to
               me still, I am puzzled with affection.
               He lay now, rasping breaths, punk to a system
               more concerned with bed space than with healing.
               Is there a less ennobling sphere of passage
               than this dull chrome and linen house of numbness?
               White smocks pass through; like me they only wait.
               I do not blame them for their helplessness,
               though their officious posturing revolts.
               Gloved, the attendants turn him gingerly
               and adjust the hissing nozzle in his mouth.
               Ashen, diminished-to-bone, unconscious thing,
               he seems a hatchling fallen from its nest.
               I would cup it in my hands, and running
               to the house shout, "Mother! Look what I have found!"

CHORUS: Praise brief horror which is the death of dying.

STRAIGHT BROTHER: But she would not be there, nor anyone else,
               only he as a small boy, reading his book.
               He would stare into my hands, then look up
               and smile a worried smile into my eyes.
               Together we would fashion a cotton nest
               and keep it, a day or two, between our beds.

THE CONVERSION

MALE CHORUS: All thought is music played upon the nerves.

FEMALE CHORUS: All prayer is music played upon the nerves.

MALE CHORUS: All prayer is thought to medicate the mind.

FEMALE CHORUS: All thoughts are prayers to details bound by time.

MALE CHORUS: Details are icons to the wakeful senses.

FEMALE CHORUS: All thought is music played upon the nerves.

MALE CHORUS: All prayer is music played upon the nerves.

FEMALE
CHORUS LEADER: His room of sixteen years remains the same.
Slick posters in which music raptures freeze,
or naked air-brushed women slink and pose
line the walls, and adolescent clutter
is mirror of his adolescent mind.
But he is different than the boy I knew
even a month ago; his core is changed.
When he speaks, and he rarely does, his eyes
seem fixed upon a distant thing, something
beyond familiar walls, familiar life,
and his voice, still webbed with brief hormonal cracks,
seems haunted by a calm no boy should feel.
I searched his room for contraband, thought surely

the change was caused by drugs, but found nothing
a mother hunting horrors should expect.
Instead of needles, pills, white powder, pipes
or baggies stuffed with vegetation, all
I found that startled was a Bible, thumbed
and crinkled through and through from use, pages
dog-eared, many passages marked with red.

MALE CHORUS:　　　　Praise those who ride across the desert skies
in hushed balloons, or scale white peaks to breathe
a thinner, pristine air, and scan horizons.

FEMALE CHORUS:　　　Praise those who seek stark heights from which to see.

MALE CHORUS:　　　　Belief a heart seeks out is sacrosanct.

FEMALE CHORUS:　　　Belief hard-earned is holy in itself.

MALE
CHORUS LEADER:　　　I pegged him brighter than he seemed, and tests
have proved my estimation solid; he scored
a dozen points or more above the norm
in all the categories but a few
in which he hovered somewhere near the mean.
And yet he is a classic low achiever.
He dreams beyond my voice in class, beyond
the daily task or topic of discussion.
This morning, though, I tried to coax him out,
to make him yap along with all the others
regarding some bleak issue of the day,
encourage him to join in our Socratic
blather through a topic on which most kids
ape their daddies' dinner-table passions.
His calm reply to whether one should live
if breathing means mere breath entangled in
an apparatus that compels each one,
whether a life prolonged by artifice
is worthy of our lives, was brief and measured.

He said salvation is the only issue,
and that no life is life unless it's saved.
At first I didn't understand; I thought
he meant by "saved" preserved, maintained, extended.
But soon it was apparent what he meant.
The kids grew hushed, beyond embarrassment,
as he who otherwise is like them all
in every other detail of their lives
explained from midst of eerie calm how life
is sacred only as a gift to God.
He quoted scripture, glowed as if enraptured,
and finished off the hour by asking all
around, including me, if Jesus lives
within our hearts. But no one spoke or moved,
until the brutal bell ran up our spines.

FEMALE CHORUS: Praise emptiness that signifies itself.

MALE CHORUS: Beware the bloody nest and bloody hive.

FEMALE CHORUS: Praise simple resolutions in the night.

MALE CHORUS: Praise promises of deities we dream.

FEMALE CHORUS: Beware the promise that we cannot hear.

FEMALE
CHORUS LEADER: If he were simply reaching out to those
who live in faith, if he were only seeking
such fellowship among the faithful as
he once had sought approval of his peers,
I wouldn't feel alarm; I'd wait it out.
But he has changed with no apparent help.
It is his own volition uninfluenced
by another human will that transforms

him from a boy engrossed by television,
obnoxious music and fantasies of sex
into a quiet Bible-reading stranger.
This morning as I cleaned his room I found
an Etch-a-Sketch he'd played with as a child.
He'd fetched it from the sack of childhood stuff
I hide, too poorly, from myself and him
between the drier and the old fuse box.
He'd doodled on the plastic screen a cross,
then under it wrote JESUS DIED FOR ALL
OUR SINS. How may evil be an issue
for one whose world is filled with loving care?
He's never read the paper or watched the news,
and what he knows of horror is from movies.
What sins may such a boy need saving from?

MALE CHORUS: Awareness of the horrors of the world
                     will change a gentle sunset into carnage.

MALE
CHORUS LEADER: It isn't the fact of faith I must dismiss,
                     but rather that a boy, whose heart will boil
                     for years in sexual want, may suddenly
                     transform into the tranquil host of it.

FEMALE CHORUS: Beware the calm allure of certainty.

MALE CHORUS: Praise hearts that seek the calm of certainty.

MALE
CHORUS LEADER: This morning when I told the kids to pass
                     their essays forward, I noticed that he slipped
                     a single hand-scrawled page onto the pile
                     of laser-printed, neatly stacked and stapled,
                     half-plagerized ghost-written tomes on topics
                     as obscene to adolescent minds as doom.
                     I plucked it out and glanced at it, and when
                     the bell had freed them from my will, and the hall
                     seethed with loud and clumsy longings, I read

his prayer that I should one day know his God,
and felt disgust that changed, that night, to envy.
For as I lay, a little crunk and horny,
alone, divorced and childless, prospects dim,
the smell of TV dinners and unwashed clothes
small scars upon the dark, I wept an hour
for nothing, and for my life, which are the same.
But then, as always, I thought of piles of shoes;
and naked children herded into rooms;
and people, naked, scratching walls and ceiling
as the gas ate the air and screams collapsed
into the hissing of the gas, and I
could only laugh at such a clumsy God,
such a clumsy, clownish God who will gild
the hearts of innocent fools with peace, and rip
the will to decency from hearts of men
who thrill then to the suffering of the mild.
I rose and paced the room, switched on the light,
and read the prayer again, and laughed out loud,
angry at the pompous little prig,
and at myself for envying a fool.

FEMALE CHORUS: Beware the wings of angels dipped in blood.
                        Beware the angels with the bleeding tongues.
                        Beware the angels with a taste for blood.

MALE CHORUS: Praise angels swarming over human carnage.

FEMALE
CHORUS LEADER: By his conversion I am forced to fix
                        upon my own life's faithlessness, though I
                        believe belief is relative to words,
                        that paradise, damnation, and all zones
                        in between shimmer at the ends of words,
                        where thought dissolves, disperses, fades away.
                        I rise each sunrise and pray by every task,
                        every boring duty performed by rote.
                        The details of my life are beads for prayers,
                        and prayer is all but self-annihilation.
                        All deity is rank condition, rank
                        inviability of all our lives

in time, and nature is the laughter of
all matter at itself hysterically.
I wish my child serenity of faith
as long as it is free of righteousness,
for the righteous are the scourge of common sense,
and life is sacred only in its common
aspects as sense is common to the tribe.
Let shaman shake his gourd above the child
and think the ceremony cleansing rite.
The mother washing infant nightly will
be organismic rite more wonderful.
Today, as he was gathering up his things
for school, I grabbed and hugged him hard and kissed
his forehead as when he was a little boy.
I held his face and stared into his eyes.
His tranquility was real, and also real
the distance, the soulful distance from his life
to mine, and real the passion of his faith.
I smiled at him and let him go, and wept.

FEMALE CHORUS: Beware the transformations of a child.

MALE CHORUS: Beware the transformations of a child.

FEMALE CHORUS: Beware the strangers children may become.

MALE CHORUS: Praise monsters whom we hold, and love, and fear.

MALE
CHORUS LEADER: Two thousand years ago, perhaps a man
gave breath to sentiments that were not new,
yet may have seemed so coming from his mouth.
His role was conjured by collective will:
he stepped into a social breach; it closed
behind him; now and since he has been trapped
there, only dust, and yet the medium
for propaganda odious and divine.
That little rabbi's reputation grew,

transformed, inflated, accrued such epic heft
it is the massive rock before his tomb,
unmovable as human trepidation.
It seems so Jewish that a Jew should vex
the very nature of the Jewish mind:
that human artifice of unity
shattered and reconfigured every day
by habits of reflection and regard
determined by a history of despair.

MALE CHORUS: Praise humble longings of the humble man.

FEMALE CHORUS: Beware the man who thinks himself a god.
                   Beware the god who claims a humble aspect.

MALE CHORUS: Praise bright psychosis of the faithful mind.

FEMALE
CHORUS LEADER: I've lost my child to hope in miracles,
                   to stories of impossible achievements.
                   All faith is testimony to a lie,
                   a lie as necessary as the rain,
                   and one in which belief is blossom of
                   the will to subjugate the flesh to dreams.

FEMALE CHORUS: Praise mild corruptions for the sake of love.

MALE
CHORUS LEADER: If God is love, then God, too, is corrupt.
                   But God of fathers, father God, is love
                   imagined for the sake of heart-felt pity,
                   a condition possible but when one feels
                   abstracted from the misery of life.

MALE CHORUS: Beware reduction of miraculous
                   events, real or imagined, to fear of death.

FEMALE CHORUS:	Beware the heart that does not yearn for wonder.
MALE CHORUS LEADER:	I splash cheap whiskey over ice, flip on the television, watch weather maps bleed their sacred prophesies across the screen, as head of cheerful prophet speaks in tongues of fronts and systems and the faithful moon. I shall expire upon a lake of fire, between commercials for deodorants.
FEMALE CHORUS:	Praise gray affections of the ironist. Praise heaven which is void of irony.
MALE CHORUS:	There is no greater truth than irony.
FEMALE CHORUS LEADER:	My child, my fool, my love abandons me. I wish him sweet, safe passage on the ship of faith, across the sea of nothingness.